Advent in the First Person

Advent in the First Person

Brian Durand
Carolyn Wirtz Poelstra

ISBN: 979-8-218-55226-8

Scripture quotations in this publication, unless otherwise indicated, are from the New International Version (2011). BibleGateway.com. http://www.biblegateway.com/versions/

Book Cover by Bobby Strickland

First Printing, 2024

*Thank you to everyone who made this book a reality.
Special thanks to the readers who offered edits, ideas,
and, without fail, encouragement.*

*Thank you to all who attend Clay Church.
You were our inspiration and reason for writing.*

*Thank you to Bobby Strickland for the incredible, original
painting that graces the cover.*

*And special thanks to our families. When you wondered why we
hadn't come to bed yet, this is what we were doing.*

CONTENTS

INTRODUCTION

ENTER THE STORY

I was in college when I realized there isn't an innkeeper in the Biblical account of the birth of Jesus. I'd read the story in the gospels of Luke and Matthew multiple times, but I also had seen Christmas pageants and dramatic interpretations of the Christmas story. These presentations always had an innkeeper, either sad and apologetic or impatient and rude, who told Joseph, with Mary sitting on the donkey nearby, that there wasn't any room in the inn. Perhaps this is a statement of my own investment in Bible study at the time, but I easily melded the stories together in my mind. There wasn't room in the inn, so there must have been an innkeeper to share this news.

The absence of the innkeeper in the story came with other revelations for me about the Biblical account of the birth of Jesus, and what we've added over time in our cultural telling through hymns and Christmas pageants. For example, there was no mention of a donkey for Mary to sit on. Many scholars believe she would have walked. Nor does the Bible identify three wise men. The wise men bring three gifts – gold, frankincense, and myrrh – but there could have been three or 30 wise people. We don't know. And while I love the lullaby of "Away in the Manger," and sang it to my children when they were little, the Bible says nothing of cattle lowing nor that Jesus didn't cry.

Fast forward to a few years ago. One Sunday in Advent I began my sermon with what I thought would be a fun quiz on the Biblical account of the Christmas story. My intention that day was to use the quiz to grab everyone's attention, and

1

then offer a Gospel message of hope as I preached. The quiz did, indeed, grab everyone's attention. However, after worship, no one remembered anything I said after the quiz, and some were visibly shaken.

"How did I not know there wasn't an innkeeper in the Bible?" one younger woman asked me.

"I've always believed there were three wise men," an older man said. "I don't know the Bible very well, but I thought I knew the story of the birth of Jesus. I've heard it enough times."

Then an older woman, one of the true saints of the church, came up to me with tears in her eyes. "I think I need to go back and read my Bible," she said. "After years of Bible study, how do I still know so little?"

I worried for a day or two about the after-effects of the quiz. I hadn't intended for anyone to feel bad, let alone cry. Then, on Wednesday that week, I received an email from the same older woman.

"Dear Pastor Brian,

...I want to thank you for the Christmas quiz on Sunday. I didn't do very well, and found myself kind of emotional about it. So I went back and read the Bible, and then I realized I hadn't read the story myself in years. I heard it read in worship and just thought I knew it. Reading it through myself, I saw again that there wasn't an innkeeper, but then I also began to wonder how a pregnant woman can't find a place to stay. Wouldn't someone move out to make room? And I thought about Mary walking all that distance, while pregnant. The story became even more profound for me when I read and paid

2

attention to the details. Thanks for challenging us to read and learn the story at another level."

After reading this kind, faithful woman's note, I realized that anything we can do to immerse ourselves more deeply in the story, to learn from God's word with an eye to every detail within the context, is worthwhile. Yes, the songs, the plays, and the books about the Nativity take creative license to help tell the most powerful and engaging story of God's love. Yet they do so to invite the hearer, the seer, and the reader to more thoroughly explore and more realistically experience this gift of God becoming human and walking among us. Were there cattle lowing? We can't say for sure, but there were certainly animals around. Was there a somewhat mean innkeeper? Probably not, but we should ask why no one would help a pregnant woman.

The pages ahead might best be classified as historical fiction, yet they are rooted in the study of the Nativity story of the Gospel accounts and include a deep dive into the context of the time of the birth of Jesus. These first-person accounts are shared to convey historical and Biblical context, to make us think about God and the birth of Jesus, and to make us think about our faith. My hope and prayer in sharing these written stories now is the same as it was when I first shared these accounts in our congregation as a sermon series during Advent. I pray that these narratives will encourage each person to take a deeper look at the Biblical story, ask questions, and seek God's wisdom and truth.

Let me encourage you now, before you read the pages ahead, to examine the accounts of the birth of Jesus in the gospels of Luke and Matthew. As you read, pay attention to what is there, to what Matthew and Luke want the hearers and readers of their accounts to know. And pay attention to what is not there, the questions the text raises for you, details that you'd like to know. Bookmark this page, and when you've read the accounts in the Bible, come back and pick up your reading here.

Now receive this invitation to enter the story of the birth of Jesus in a new way. Imagine that these characters of the Biblical account aren't just statues in a nativity set, but flesh and blood people with life stories, sharing their experiences with you. Imagine you're encountering them in the streets of Bethlehem, in the fields of Judea, as you look for a room in Bethlehem, or arrive to pray at the Temple. May these accounts open your eyes to see the birth of Jesus anew, and to turn back to the Biblical account with fresh perspective and deeper historical and contextual understanding of the time of the birth of Jesus.

- Brian

CHAPTER 1

HERE I AM
ISAIAH

Prophecy is a lonely and painful vocation. I feel every sin, every transgression, every injustice in the very seat of my bones. I see what God sees, and my heart breaks. God speaks, and I hear, and I share what I hear. And no one wants to hear it.

I didn't grow up dreaming of this job – being a prophet, I mean. At least, not exactly. In the year that King Uzziah died, I had a vision. I saw the LORD seated on a throne. Angels with six wings were gathered around singing, "Holy, holy, holy is the Lord Almighty; the whole earth is full of his glory." It was magnificent, and terrifying. I feared for my life. I'd been taught that if you see the face of God, you don't live to tell about it. I could feel everything wrong with me in that moment - the weight of my sin, my unholiness, every mistake. Who was I to have this experience?

In response to the vision, I said something about my unworthiness, and then I heard the voice of the Lord saying, "Whom shall I send? And who will go for us?"

Before I knew it, I answered, "Here am I. Send me!" I didn't plan to say it, in the sense that I thought it through and said yes. The words just came out. And I became a prophet.

My first assignment: God sent me to share words that God's people would ignore. Literally, that's what God told me. I was instructed to tell people they wouldn't listen and their hearts would harden. How is that for a fun assignment? When I asked how long, God said until the people were carried away from our cities and our kingdom was destroyed. Did I mention that being a prophet is lonely? Who would sign up for a job where you tell people what they don't want to hear, get rejected, and then watch as the calamity you warned of comes to pass?

People sometimes don't understand what a prophet is. A prophet is not someone who predicts the future. There are fortune tellers in some leaders' inner circles of advisors who claim to know the future, but that isn't my role. And I'll be direct: I'm not so sure how accurate or honest these fortune-telling advisors are. They seem to be most concerned with saying what the leader wants to hear. I find myself saying the opposite more often.

A prophet speaks God's word and is a messenger for God, even when the message is hard to hear. We share with leaders what God tells us; we speak to the people of what God shows us. We speak of the consequences of our unfaithfulness even when the leaders threaten us. We speak of injustice even when people curse us. Want to know something even more wild? Sometimes God asks us to send a message in the very names we give our children. I have a son named Shear-jashub which literally means "the remaining few will return." The name God gave us for my son is, in itself, a message of hope from God.

All this is to say, as prophets we may speak of what the future holds, warn of what will happen if we stay on the current path, but our message – my message on behalf of God – is for today, for this people in this time. For example, during the reign of King Ahaz in Judah, Aram and Israel formed an alliance and set out to attack Jerusalem, our capital. God sent me with my son to King Ahaz to deliver a message. I was to tell King Ahaz not to be afraid, and instruct him to ask God for a sign that God would deliver Judah. King Ahaz refused to ask for the sign, so God gave me a sign to give him anyway. I was instructed to say, "The young woman is pregnant and is about to give birth to a son, and she will name him Immanuel." Immanuel means God with us. God was inviting Ahaz to trust God's presence and God's plan. He didn't.

Ahaz isn't the only one not to trust. God's people still aren't listening or paying attention to what God is saying or doing. Many are living quite comfortable lives in Judah. The economic conditions are favorable; fields are full of abundance. Those with economic and social standing are adding land and second homes. They don't see any problems as they worship, celebrate the festivals, and bring their offerings to the Temple. Yet God is grieved. Too often, wealth and abundance come from the poor, from systems that take advantage of the downtrodden and cause suffering. While living in comfort, the people ignore the injustices of the systems that bring that very comfort.

To others, this kind of injustice - a business that puts profit above everything, a wage paid that isn't enough to live on, a system of interest that the poor can't escape - isn't such a big deal. To them, that's just the way the world is. To me, as a prophet, every injustice that hurts a child of God is a catastrophe, a threat to all that God holds dear. This is not the world as God intends it to be. How can we stand by and do nothing? That's why I say to the people, wash and make yourselves clean. Take your evil deeds out of my sight; stop doing wrong. Learn to do right; seek justice. Defend the oppressed. Take up the cause of the fatherless; plead the case of the widow.

"We are responsible," I say to God's people, and to those who lead us. "We haven't been the people God invites us to be."

"We did not create the problems or the pain," they reply, as though none of them are responsible. As though the downtrodden deserve to suffer. As though the poor want to starve. As though the abused bring it upon themselves. As though the very systems from which we profit aren't to blame for the injustices around us.

The people of God don't see what I know to be true. Or maybe they just refuse to look. People without food, widows without care, children without homes, violence instead of peace, an endless cycle of poverty – all of us are responsible. Not all of us are guilty of creating the conditions to begin with, but all of us are responsible for seeking God's intention and changing the systems.

What God finds so disgusting about our worship is that we're taking the time to worship with all these beautiful offerings and words, but we don't love people as God does. Not really. We don't take care of those suffering the most. Our whole world is built on systems that favor the rich and powerful. We have forgotten that God's intention is to bless all people through us. Not just us!

This is why God instructs me to address the leaders and the people, particularly those who are the people of God, with woes and warnings of what will come. I warn those who are building vast wealth, those who celebrate while others suffer, those who lie and cheat, those who ignore evil, those who are arrogant, and those who take advantage of others. I warn that this way will lead to judgment, to God bringing down the structures and powers so that the system can be reset. I remind the people that being a chosen people of God isn't about privilege and status, but about mission and responsibility.

I warn the people about God's anger. People don't like to think of God as angry. I can't fully capture God's feelings or essence, but maybe this image can help us understand a little better. Imagine you plant a vineyard with the very best vines, on the choicest land, with tremendous care, and then you share it as a gift with your children. When you return, however, you find they haven't cared for the vineyard at all, and the fruit is worthless. You're sad, and angry, not simply because the vines are bad, or even that the vineyard hasn't been cared for, but because you wanted the very best for your children and they have squandered the opportunity to thrive with the gifts you gave to them. You see, God's anger isn't vindictive. God's anger is restorative, a sign of God's desire to set things right. God wants the best for all of God's creation.

God once gave me a vision to help people understand God's desire for us. Listen to this:

> The wolf will live with the lamb,
> the leopard will lie down with the goat,
> the calf and the lion and the yearling together;
> and a little child will lead them.
> The cow will feed with the bear,
> their young will lie down together,
> and the lion will eat straw like the ox.
> The infant will play near the cobra's den,
> and the young child will put its hand
> into the viper's nest.
> They will neither harm nor destroy
> on all my holy mountain,
> for the earth will be filled
> with the knowledge of the LORD
> as the waters cover the sea.

Isn't that a beautiful image? That's what God wants for us – community, peace, safety, understanding, knowledge of God's goodness. That's what God has put on my heart to share.

To get there, however, for God to set things right, things must change. Sometimes those changes are painful, and come at a cost. Sometimes systems of injustice must be broken completely before healing or restoration can take place. These are the consequences God calls me to share with leaders, and rulers, and nations. Every leader who wins and takes power seems to believe they are divinely chosen. Then, again and again, these leaders and nations forget the truth that God raised them to be a blessing to others. They forget the power they have comes as a gift from God, who calls for justice and righteousness. Instead of leading with humility and compassion, these leaders make unjust laws, issue oppressive decrees, deprive the poor of their rights, prey on the weak, and withhold justice, all justified by a desire to destroy enemies and hold power. Communities divide, nations weaken, and then fall. This is our story, but it doesn't have to be.

All is not lost, or without hope. Yes, times are dark. And yes, things may be worse before they get better. But God is faithful. God will not stop guiding a faithful remnant toward God's desire for all of creation. And you're invited to be part of that faithful remnant.

Even as God has given me words of woe and warning for people in this day, God also has shown me what is possible, a vision of what God wants for us. I carry this promise of God in my heart, and share it these days whenever hope seems lost.

> For to us a child is born
> to us a son is given,
> and the government will be on his shoulders.

And he will be called
Wonderful Counselor, Mighty God,
Everlasting Father, Prince of Peace.
Of the greatness of his government and peace
there will be no end.
He will reign on David's throne
and over his kingdom,
establishing and upholding it
with justice and righteousness
from that time on and forever.
The zeal of the LORD Almighty
will accomplish this.

This nation will fall, as will those who follow its path of greed and the desire for power. Times will not be easy. But God will establish a kingdom that knows no end. God's kingdom will be built on justice and experienced by those who love as God loves, and led by one who does not desire power and control, but peace and righteousness.

You're invited to choose a kingdom; to choose a story. This is the invitation I bring as a prophet of God. You can choose to put your faith in the power of this nation, in its systems, and in its ways. Or you can choose to put your faith in God's kingdom. There will be suffering ahead for those who are faithful. I wish it wasn't so. But the one who stands for justice, feels the weight of the sins of the world, and takes responsibility for those who are hurting, carries a burden. God does not promise the way will be easy. God promises those who remain faithful to God's kingdom will see light even in the darkness, will find satisfaction and fulfillment, and will participate in the eternal plans of God.

Being a prophet is lonely and painful, but I wouldn't choose any other vocation. I am privileged to offer God's word to God's people, and an invitation to have faith in God's promise.

Surely God is my salvation;
I will trust and not be afraid.
The LORD, the LORD himself,
is my strength and my defense
he has become my salvation.
Give praise to the LORD, proclaim his name;
make known among the nations what he has done,
and proclaim that his name is exalted.
Sing to the LORD, for he has done glorious things;
let this be known to all the world.

I am free to speak the truth, and to testify to what God has done, what God is doing, and what God will do.

REFLECTION GUIDE & QUESTIONS

- What injustice in the world today most upsets you?

A prophet is one who speaks to the people, or to leaders, on behalf of God. The role of the prophet is extraordinarily difficult. He or she bears the responsibility of representing God to the people, and representing the people to God. He or she is called to speak the truth, even when it is difficult for others to hear, and call out injustice wherever it is found.

- Who do you think of as prophets in the world today?
- What injustices seem to be repeated from society to society and from generation to generation?

Isaiah presents several lists of woes and warnings, and no nation seems left out. He shares that people hurting from injustice grieves God, and that those who take advantage of people who are suffering or hurting make God angry.

- Where do you see people hurting or being taken advantage of today?
- In what ways do some of the comforts, security, and opportunities we have today come at the expense of others?
- What can make it difficult, or hold us back, from confronting causes of suffering or systems of injustice today?
- How does our response to injustice and suffering in our community express to others our understanding of God?

As Christians reading the Old Testament prophets through the lens of Jesus, we see how their words describe who Jesus is. But Isaiah, and the other prophets, weren't asking people to simply wait for Jesus to come. They were speaking to people and leaders in a particular time and place, inviting them to understand who God is, see what God is doing, and respond in faith. The prophets invited the people to see their role and responsibility, and to trust God.

- What do you see God doing in our midst right now?
- How can you trust in God even when things seem to be falling apart?

CHAPTER 2

EXPECTING MIRACLES
ZECHARIAH

How do you trust when everything seems to be stacked against you? How do you trust when you feel like your prayers are unanswered, your hopes dashed?

"Zechariah," my dad would say all the time when I was growing up, "trust in the Lord with all your heart, and lean not on your own understanding."

My father was always quoting from the Holy Scriptures. If I'd get a little sassy with Mom, he'd quickly say, "I think the Scriptures say to honor your mother, Zechariah."

In tough times for our family or our community, Dad would say at dinner, "Isaiah says, 'The Redeemer will come to Zion, to those in Jacob who repent of their sins, thus says the Lord.'"

"God's promise is real," Dad would tell us next. "We just have to expect God to show up. We have to have faith."

But as much as Dad quoted from the Holy Scriptures, we all knew his favorite verse was from the wisdom of Proverbs.

"Trust in the Lord with all your heart, and lean not on your own understanding."

Dad said that so much, that by the time I was a teenager he'd just say "trust," and I knew the rest. If I was getting angry at my siblings, Dad would say "trust," and "in the Lord" would finish in my head as I suddenly knew I shouldn't act out my anger. If I was beginning to get frustrated with a task, Dad would whisper, "Zechariah, trust," and I'd know he was telling me to stop worrying so much and put whatever was holding me back in God's hands.

"Trust in the Lord with all your heart, and lean not on your own understanding." That instruction, with the power of my Dad's voice, seemed so simple when I was a kid.

Then I grew up. I was, of course, destined to be a priest. I was a Levite, of the tribe of Abijah.

"Right here in the Holy Scripture," my dad would say, "we find our duty to the people, to the land, and to the Temple."

He meant in the book of Chronicles, where it says King David appointed our family line to the priesthood. Finding your family name right there in the Holy Scriptures is a strange and powerful feeling.

"It is our honor and duty to God," Dad would say with a gleam in his eye. I was trained, really from birth, in the priestly duties. I knew the Holy Scriptures by heart. I cared for the community. I served where I was appointed.

And then I met Elizabeth - beautiful, kind, faithful Elizabeth. I am so blessed to be married to her. She is also of the tribe of Levi, so she understands the priestly call. In case you're now asking the "marrying within your own family" question, I should add: Elizabeth is from a whole different family tree. Hundreds of years of ancestry and branches of that tree lie between us.

Anyway, Elizabeth was raised in a home similar to mine, following the Torah, observing the Holy Days, living true to God's instructions. She is so faithful. Probably more than me. Nothing could shake her faith, not even our inability to have children.

We tried everything – we prayed, we sought the advice of the wise elders, we listened to the ideas of the midwives. We prayed some more. For some reason, we just weren't blessed with a child of our own. At first, we thought a child would come in time. And then we began to feel the stigma. People would whisper as we passed by. Rumors of our lack of faith or lack of righteousness would leak back to our family. "God is not with them," people would say behind our backs. And in those moments, I'd hear my father's voice encouraging me as it echoed in my head. "Trust in the Lord, Zechariah!"

"How?" I wanted to scream back.

Some people say you lose faith in a moment of doubt or struggle. But I don't think so. I think faith can sort of seep away, one loss or one doubt at a time. A painful experience that leaves you asking, "Why me?" without a clear answer. A hurtful word from someone in your circle of friends. Seeing hypocrisy in leaders of your community. Someone telling you that God has removed God's blessing from you. At least that was my experience. Don't get me wrong, I hadn't stopped believing in God. That was never in doubt for me. But I lost faith that God would show up. I stopped expecting God to show up. I kept going through the motions, but I did so without belief that God could do miracles, without any real trust in divine promises.

And then, a day came that changed everything. I remember it so clearly.

You should know that entering the holy place of the Temple is the experience of a lifetime. And by experience of a lifetime, I literally mean most priests only do it once in their lifetime. There are over 15,000 priests, in divisions by family, and each division serves a couple of weeks each year. My family, Abijah, has around 350 priests in it alone. When our time came to serve, we would draw lots to determine our appointment for the two weeks of the year we served. Only five of the 350 would serve in the Temple itself, looking after the lamp and the altar of incense. So, imagine my surprise to learn that I would be serving for a week not outside, but within the Temple itself. I could imagine my dad seeing this day and saying, "Zechariah, this is the highest duty and honor." As I said, this was to be the experience of a lifetime.

That particular day was already loaded with meaning, and my role was to enter the Holy Place to burn incense on behalf of the people. The worshippers had gathered and remained in the outer court, while I went into the Temple to the golden altar, the altar of incense. I entered with trepidation. Only the High Priest on the day of atonement goes any closer to the Holy of Holies. My burning of incense would carry the prayers of the people closer to God.

And these prayers, they mattered. Life under Roman occupation was not easy. You played the games and gave your allegiance to the local appointees of the Empire, or you suffered. Even the Temple, the most sacred of places, and the priesthood were not free of Roman politics. Herod was appointed "King of the Jews" by the Roman Senate, but his kingdom was a far cry from the shalom, the peace, promised by our God. It was a kingdom where the poor were taxed to starvation to pay for Herod's building projects. The prayers of the people, prayers for deliverance, for the kingdom God promised, for the messiah – they mattered.

So, there I knelt and prayed. I prayed the prayers that I'd been taught from birth: the traditional prayers of our faith. I praised God; I prayed God would return us to lives based in the Torah; I prayed for forgiveness of our sins; I prayed for the kingdom of David to be restored; I prayed for God to send the messiah. I prayed and prayed knowing I stood in a long line of continuous and focused prayer.

As I prayed, I looked up, and there stood a man. "He shouldn't be here," I thought, followed immediately by, "Wait. He didn't come in. I would have seen him." But there he was, right next to me, standing at the right side of the altar of incense. There was something about him, something powerful, yet familiar. I really don't have the words, even now, but inside I knew. He was an angel, a messenger. And I was terrified. I wasn't worthy of this. I wasn't faithful enough for this. This was too big. Too important. I could not even comprehend his presence. Yet there he was, appearing to me. His first words, I'll never forget them: "Do not be afraid, Zechariah. Your prayer has been heard."

My prayer had been heard? Later, people would say that God heard my prayer for a son. But it's odd to me, as that wasn't my prayer on that particular day. I was old. Elizabeth was old. Sure, we had prayed and prayed for God to send a child to bless our lives. But at some point we'd resigned ourselves to the truth that we wouldn't have children. My prayer that day was for the people. For deliverance. For the messiah. And then the angel said, your prayer has been answered. Did he mean a messiah?

After that, the angel said this: "Your wife Elizabeth will bear you a son."

"What? You must have the wrong priest, my friend." I'm not too proud to say I just couldn't process how any of this could be happening, and I must admit I got a bit hung up at that moment. My brain just couldn't comprehend this news. The rest of the encounter is more or less a blur. The angel said we were to name our son John, or literally, "God is gracious." And then he said my son, John, would be great, would be celebrated by many. He said my son would bring many back to the Lord, that he would speak with the power and spirit of Elijah. My son!

And then he said this – this part I heard: he said that my son would get people ready for the Lord's coming. He would prepare the way for the Lord, the Messiah.

In response to all of that, do you know what I said? Surely something profound and humble, you might think.

No. I said, "How can I be sure of this?"

That's what I said. To an angel. An angel had appeared in front of me, and yet my faith was still shaky. I still couldn't grasp that God would fulfill God's promises. Particularly through me.

That's when I felt it. Suddenly my voice was just gone. It wasn't painful or anything. It was as though the part of me that makes sound had just disappeared. Nothing. No words. The angel then introduced himself.

"I'm Gabriel," he said as he told me I'd be unable to speak until the child was born and named.

Elizabeth will probably tell you it did me good to just have to listen for nine months. She would be right, though it didn't start well. The people were waiting outside. How do you pantomime that you saw an angel who said you are going to have a baby even as an old man? There is no way to communicate that via signs and gestures. Truthfully, I don't think I could have communicated it with words. Still, the people outside knew something had happened. I just couldn't find a way to tell them.

And maybe that's okay. For five months, Elizabeth and I didn't tell anyone. We were so fearful. Excited, but fearful. And then Mary came to visit. She was pregnant, and had told her family that an angel had appeared to her, telling her she would give birth to the Son of God, the Messiah. The family thought it best for her to come stay with us, and with our own miracle at hand, we were so glad to welcome her. As she arrived, her very presence caused our baby to leap in Elizabeth's womb. Well, I'll let Elizabeth tell you more about that.

You might think nine months of silence would be awful. There were tough moments, for certain. We communicated as best we could, and I tried to be helpful. Mainly I observed. And as I observed, I realized how much I had been missing. God was showing up every day. I just hadn't been paying attention. God would show up in the morning, casting the created beauty of the morning sunrise. God would show up as people turned the focus of their lives back to God during their pilgrimage to make offerings at the Temple. God was showing up in the love that held Elizabeth and me together through the trials of our lives. God hadn't abandoned us. I just wasn't looking, or expecting God to show up. I couldn't see past my personal story to the bigger story God was writing. So, until that day in the Temple, I didn't see God's presence.

By the time our baby, John, was born, I could see again. I couldn't talk, but I sure could see. I began to expect God to show up. I counted on God's promises. God is gracious. That's the meaning of the name I had been given for my son. When the name John was given, I found my voice and I sang. I sang my praise. I sang of how God was showing up right now. I sang of God's promises of mercy and love. I sang of salvation and hope. I sang that the Messiah was coming. I wanted everyone to know that God is true to God's promises.

The world will challenge your faith. Painful experiences will leave you asking, why me? People, even those who are a part of your faith community, will say hurtful things. Leaders will sometimes be hypocrites. Someone may even tell you that God has removed His blessing from you. To all this I say: Don't believe it. Don't lose faith. Expect God to show up. God is already showing up - even when you can't see it. God is gracious. God is true to God's promises.

"Trust in the Lord with all your heart, and lean not on your own understanding." My father was wise.

REFLECTION GUIDE & QUESTIONS

- What is the most amazing thing you have ever witnessed?

An audience in Biblical times hearing the story of Elizabeth and Zechariah would notice that their barrenness didn't fit the widespread belief that somehow God's blessings were given to the righteous or worthy and withheld from those who strayed or were unworthy. Childbirth was seen as a blessing for the righteous. Elizabeth and Zechariah would have been judged by society because they couldn't bear children.

- Do you think you have to be righteous or worthy to receive God's blessings? Why or why not?

This story can be extremely difficult for those who have experienced or are experiencing infertility. Why doesn't God answer the prayers of all who are infertile? Zechariah was in the Temple to pray on behalf of the people of God, for forgiveness and deliverance. This is the prayer answered. This isn't simply someone hearing the individual answer they want from God. In this passage, God has heard the prayers of God's people for a messiah to deliver them and is sending a son to Zechariah and Elizabeth whose role will be to prepare the way.

- In your experience, how does God answer prayer?
- How have you witnessed God doing things beyond imagination?

Zechariah doubted at first. The announcement of a son for him and his wife was an expectation that seemed beyond reach.

- What doubts do you sometimes struggle with in your life of faith?
- Do you think there are consequences when we don't trust God? If yes, what are they for you?

In the birth of his child, Zechariah's doubt is transformed into prophecy. His song isn't about what has happened, but what he sees God doing in the future.

- What do you see God doing in the world right now and in the future?
- If you were going to write a song of praise to God, what would you include?
- What is one way you can commit to living with a sense of expectation?

CHAPTER 3

PURE JOY
ELIZABETH

Joy. I smile when I just think of that word. It's something so simple and yet so powerful, something brushing up against inexplicable. Joy. Something you can't explain until you yourself are surrounded by it: a mysteriously-rich harvest after a drought, the sun after weeks of rain, the best wine after being parched with thirst. The birth of a baby who you adamantly prayed for, hoped for, longed for – and yet had accepted would never come to be.

When I married Zechariah, I knew he would be a good father just as his father was before him. Zechariah's father taught him all he needed to know to be a good man. Zechariah is patient, soft, wise. He is secure in his faith and trusts in God. Just like my family, Zechariah was raised a Levite, and just like my father, he grew up to become a member of the priesthood. When I learned my father had pledged me to be married to Zechariah, I was excited because I knew we would have a lot in common. We would never run out of things to talk about! For me, our betrothal didn't feel like the passing of a woman from the father to the husband, but a smart, intellectual match. Zechariah knew the Holy Scriptures and he helped to ground me in the moments of our lives that were void of the joy that helps make life worth living. I, too, grew up in a home with the Scriptures being tossed around as part of everyday conversation; one of my favorites came from the psalms: "Weeping may stay for the night, but in the morning, joy."

"Weeping may stay for the night, but in the morning, joy."

This psalm became the heartbeat and the foundation of my adult years, the undercurrent of so many prayers that I uttered between gritted teeth and choking wails month after month for decades. In the midst of looking for joy in the morning – every morning – I, on my most sorrowful days, would alter the prayer just a little: "but in the *mourning*... joy." In this simple little prayer, an act of submission to God. God, help me to find joy even in the midst of this grief.

And the mourning was steadfast. Not too long after Zechariah and I were married, we hoped to have a baby. Soon I start to track my bleeding with the phases of the moon and, as it wanes into a smaller and smaller sliver, I start to hold my breath, grip a hand against my womb, lift that lifeline to the God who hears my prayers: "Oh God. In the morning... joy?" What I notice after months of staring at the sky, watching the moon, is that it is always when the moon is at its smallest, right before it disappears for a night, that I begin to birth agony crimson yet again. I cry; the pain is too real. Where do I find joy in this mourning? I wonder. This pain is in my body and the pain is in my soul. And yet I allow myself to grip that sliver of light the Lord still holds above us. On these nights, I would wrap my arms around my shoulders, imagining God is holding me there in the curve of the moon, that I am nestled against its breast.

The moon waxes, wanes, disappears entirely. The noon, the night, the morning. The growing season comes and goes.

We and our neighbors grow grapes and olives and figs and barley and wheat and beans, enough for the survival of an entire community. The girls in our village grow up and move into their husband's house; by the next growing season, they swell at the abdomen or strap a baby to their backs. With each passing growing season, each passing harvest, and each passing year, I give thanks to God for the fertility of our land. I am grateful for fertile soil and a fruitful earth even though my own body doesn't bear fruit. These things are all so natural, I realize. The moon bulges and narrows; wheat spreads its seeds, whither, and die; grapevines are harvested and cut away; women get married and have babies. This is the way the world works. This is God-divine order. I keep seeking and finding joy in all of these details, in all the ways in which God is present, even in the absence and the emptiness.

This longing for a child I have never known, one who has never been a reality; this grief over an empty belly and empty arms comes and goes in waves of sadness. I find some parts of this natural order are just so much harder than others. Even this grief, though, is punctuated by joy. This grief reminds me of the moon, dark for a night but the next night, light. In the morning, joy. Harvest: a reminder of my own barrenness. And yet: joy in God's provision. Seeing a young bride's belly expand with new life, hearing birth cries from mother and babe, seeing that new life presented in worship to God forty days later. This grief over what I am missing. And yet: joy in what God is creating and how God keeps on working. I hold this tension in my own body, the thin veil that separates joy from despair being the love of God, pulling me ever more passionately into its orbit. In the morning, joy. In the mourning, joy.

Zechariah, in his goodness, does not turn away from me. He has every reason and every right to divorce me. That's just how the laws work. My husband can divorce me for any reason, and especially now that I have caused shame to him and his family. We both know what people say: that we have fallen out of favor with God; that God has removed God's blessing from us. Maybe we're not so favored after all. To save his reputation and his family bloodline, Zechariah could divorce me and remarry another woman, one who might give him children. I wouldn't blame him if he did. I would be left to a life of poverty. No man would ever marry me: I have already laid with a man and everyone know I can't have children. This is just the way things are, and the law is on the husband's side.

And yet, despite all of these things, there is joy. In the morning, joy. In the mourning… joy. Each day, I ask God to keep holding me close, not to abandon me in my weeping. My name, Elizabeth, has a meaning that is special to me. It means, "pledged to God." This meaning is important and beautiful. It also means, "God is my oath," and giving up myself and my future in an oath to God became the only thing I could cling to. Over these years of infertility, I have learned to accept it, as painful and as empty as it is some days. I feel the stares boring like holes into my back everywhere I go. The whispers from my neighbors burn my ears and my neck and my face with embarrassment. In these moments, I think of Zechariah. Soft, kind, compassionate Zechariah. I wonder how much the pain is magnified, to be a member of the priesthood and not have his own sons and daughters.

I try to hold fast to joy. In the morning, joy. I tell God in my prayers I will devote myself to service, not in exchange for a child but instead of one. I promise that as long as Zechariah is a priest, I will faithfully serve alongside him in the Temple in whatever ways I can. I vow to keep my head covered and follow every law and be an example to the women. While I cannot be a mother of babes, I tell God, I will be a mother of the Temple. Just as Hannah committed her longed-for son Samuel to the Temple, I will commit myself. So, I devote myself to work in the Temple in the Court of the People alongside Zechariah. I watch him closely. He smiles at me brightly when he catches me glimpsing him, just as he did when we were young and I first moved into his house and we were free to anticipate the future. I know he won't divorce me, even though he could. I can't help but wonder, sometimes, if he thinks any less of me, even though I know for certain that he loves me.

In my careful art of acceptance, I think of the Mothers who came before me. I wonder about the pain they, too, carried in their bodies, in the black void of their wombs. Sarah and Rachel. Rebekah. Hannah. These women had names. They are significant. They are our ancestors. They are a part of our rich heritage. They are evidence of God's promises fulfilled. I reflect pensively on these stories, and I wonder what promises God will fulfill for me. How are you working to surprise me? I've grown into an old woman now: I'm 88 years old. I keep about my work at home. I go to the Temple as often as I can, which is more often now that I am old and have been unprohibited by monthly bleeding for decades now. Being in the Temple is a beautiful thing. I find solace there; I find meaning there; I sense God's goodness with those of us gathered there. The mourning is steadfast, yes. It was steadfast in Sarah and Rachel and Rebekah and Hannah and it is steadfast in me. But even though mourning is steadfast, God is also steadfast. In the morning, joy.

One morning, I am preparing for Zechariah's departure to the Holy Temple where he would stay for two weeks: the priests would draw lots and Zechariah was the one God had selected to serve in the Temple. Only men could stay within the priestly quarters, so the other wives and I would keep to our homes while our husbands were gone. As I help him to gather his things, I can feel his tension bouncing off his skin between us. He is excited but also apprehensive. I would be, too, to be in the presence of God.

News, it turns out, travels at its own strange pace. While I spend two weeks at home, tending to the work around our house, our animals, and our fields in the countryside, others are coming and going from Jerusalem and the Temple there to offer sacrificial worship. Just a few days before Zechariah is scheduled to return home, while I am gathering water, a woman approaches me and says that she heard what happened to Zechariah while he was serving in the Temple. I must look puzzled or my eyes glaze over, because she says Zechariah had been in the Temple praying and something very strange happened there in the presence of God: he walked out of the Temple completely mute. Stunned, I drop the jug. It crashes against my feet. I stare at her incredulously, demanding the explanation that she cannot provide. Zechariah, what have you done?

I pace our home helplessly for several days, wondering what on earth Zechariah did to anger God so much that he would be stricken mute, unable to speak. I try to occupy my time with extra household tasks, extra care for our animals, and visits with our neighbors. Finally, the night before Zechariah's scheduled return, I wander outside our home in the dark. I look up at the sky as I did all those years ago, looking for the light of the moon to offer light to our suddenly-dark path. It is a full moon tonight, bright, full of hope. God will provide, I promise myself. I am reminded of the Holy Scriptures as I hold the moon's gaze. Weeping may last for a night.

The next morning, I wake up with a start, worried I will miss his coming. I prepare a meal, take care of our animals, gather water from the nearby well. A few hours after sunrise, I see him coming from a distance. I know that walk; I have watched it for decades now. He meets me at the threshold and I fall into his arms, weeping. Of all of the pain we have experienced, this is the worst of all, to not hear the soft voice of my sweet Zechariah. He holds me against him tightly, my tears soaking through his clothes and mine. Pulling me away but still holding me together with his eyes, my Zechariah looks into my face. His eyes are shiny but not with tears. This is something I don't understand.

We share bewildered glances with one another: Mine a look of confusion and his, something else I can't quite place. Looking around us, Zechariah finally picks up a stone and writes in the dirt outside our home: child. I furrow my brow at him. What does this mean? He grins at me. That old smile that I have loved since we were practically children, newly married, with nothing but hope in front of us. He bends back over. Writes slowly in the sand. "You and me. Child. Angel told me." He stands back up, presses his wrinkled up hand over my womb, waits for me to read the message. I stare at the ground. I can feel my heartbeat in my ears. My head starts spinning. I feel my mouth open in shock. Now I, too, am mute, but not in the way Zechariah is. How can this be? I look at Zechariah. He is giddy with joy. And I believe him. I believe, after all of the pain, God has answered my most fervent prayer. In the morning, joy.

Month after month, I watch the moon, just as I did as a young woman, but this time with a newfound anticipation. I admire how it grows round each month as I, too, begin to expand in my middle, stretching further and further towards this mysterious promise. I cradle this new joy in the palms of my hands, gazing up at the sky with newfound happiness. Jehovah Rapha – the One who Heals – has done this according to the Divine plan, I whisper to myself, a broad smile covering my face and burning in my heart. I am an old woman with most of her life behind her, and yet God has chosen to answer this prayer. Surely I am not worthy of this. I know God has done this out of deep love. I wonder what else God will do to surprise me, to surprise all of us. God is faithful and true to God's promises. Joy is this incredible knowing that God is using me – using us – to share God's love and purpose.

A few months later, I learn from my relatives my cousin Mary is expecting a child, and I am shocked – shocked with amazement and wonder and intrigue. I have a sense that God is using Mary, a virgin and just a girl, in surprising ways. I wonder again how God is working in the midst of our own inverted worlds. I, who had been barren all my life, and now pregnant with a miracle child, and her, a virgin, and also, in another way, pregnant with a miracle child. How can this be?

Upon learning the news of her unplanned pregnancy, Mary's family asks for her to come stay with Zechariah and me. I, captivated by God's divine plans, agree eagerly. This is a wise decision: they say nothing good comes out of Nazareth, where Mary lives, and being an unwed mother will be difficult enough without her living there in the early stages of this pregnancy. Here in the countryside, though, we are free to move about a little more freely; she is virtually unknown here.

"Elizabeth!" Mary says breathlessly as she walks through the doorway to our house. I can see the relief settle in her eyes, see it land on her face, see it rest over her newly-swollen form.

I am sure now more than ever that she needs us. She needs to be here. She needs to be in this safe place, a place to move and a place to grow and a place to breathe. She needs us to believe this spectacular story she carries inside her.

Only a brief moment passes between us but it feels like my body is moving in slow-motion as I rush to embrace her. I am struck by the juxtaposition between the two of us: the vibrant and new held in the arms of the withered and worn. She practically collapses into my arms as I embrace this young girl who I love so much, a shared knowing between us that these next several months won't be easy for her or for her betrothed, Joseph. People will talk. They will whisper. They will in equal parts turn away from her and stare at her when they see her. I am no stranger to these experiences; I am grateful that Mary has me.

As I gather her in my arms, an incredible energy passes between us. My babe leaps in my womb, lunging towards Mary and the life growing within her, practically pulling us closer to one another. I am filled with a sense of God-given power coupled with God-given peace. Holding this power and this peace between our bodies, I know in the depths of my spirit God has intentions for these children that Mary and I cultivate with God's help. I know, somehow, Mary will bring us a Savior for the whole world, a messiah to rescue us. My child will prepare the way; Mary's child will be the way. This is the purest, deepest, most indescribable joy: to be in the presence of my Lord. In the morning, joy.

"Blessed are you among women," I exclaim through tears, wrapping Mary in my arms, "and blessed is the child you will bear!"

Mary stays with us for about three months. We talk. We laugh. We share stories. We cry and we dream. We pray: we pray about who our children will become; we pray for Mary's reception; we pray for labor and delivery and suckling. And I watch. My eyes are open with joy and delight. I am looking for joy and finding it everywhere. I watch her beautiful and capable body grow our Messiah, see her cheeks turn round and pink, watch her eyes sparkle with hope. Very soon after Mary returns home, it's time for my baby to be born, the one who will prepare the way. With Zechariah unable to speak, those at our son's circumcision and naming ceremony wanted to name him after his dad.

"No." I'm surprised at myself. My voice shakes but I hold firm. "His name will be John, for God is gracious!"

I hold my baby John against my chest, breathing in the new sweetness of his scent, tracing his wisps of soft hair against my lips. Mirroring Eve, I whisper against John's scalp, "With the help of the Lord, I have brought forth a son." I remember Rachel: "The Lord has taken away my shame." I meditate on the words spoken to Sarah: "Is anything too difficult for the Lord?" Thanks be to God for this impossible gift. This child is here, the one we had prayed so earnestly for God to give to us. The one who swam in the dark waters of my womb. The one who declared the presence of a shared Messiah. I find myself filled with awe and wonder and joy at what our Lord has done and what our Lord will do.

Joy. Knowing that God sees all of God's people in our pain and in our weeping and in our longing.

Joy. Experiencing God's unexpected but miraculous provision and healing.

Joy. Giving of ourselves to God for God's higher and holier purposes.

Joy. Experiencing the truth of God's love.

Weeping may stay for the night, I remember, leaning down to kiss my baby's cheek, but in the morning, joy.

REFLECTION GUIDE & QUESTIONS

- Reflect on a time when you felt incredible joy.

We don't know for certain that Elizabeth and Mary were cousins. The Bible only says they were relatives. What we do know is that when Mary needed to get away from the stigma and shame that family and neighbors would have shown her for being pregnant before being wed to Joseph, Elizabeth is who she turns to.

- Who do you turn to for faith-filled support in trying times?

How did Elizabeth know Mary was carrying the Christ child? Mary had just said hello to Elizabeth. Had word traveled? Did the Holy Spirit impart wisdom to Elizabeth? Whatever the case, now that Elizabeth and Mary can share this joy, the moment leads to exclamations of praise to God from them both. It's as though sharing the moment releases and heightens their experience of joy and its source: God.

- What does it feel like to be "filled with the Holy Spirit"?
- How are gratitude and joy related?

In his book *Reflections on the Psalms*, CS Lewis shares that praise completes our enjoyment, and thus the invitation to glorify God is an invitation to enjoy God.

- How does joy spread?
- What is one way you can share the gift of joy?

CHAPTER 4

I AM THE LORD'S
MARY

I breathe in, so deeply I feel that my stomach, my chest, my throat, my head have filled all the space inside of me with air. I push the air back out of my nose until it seems like there's negative space inside my body. With each breath, my feet push deeper into the ground. I close my eyes, paying attention to the soft breeze whisper across my ears, tickling the hairs that peek out from under my head scarf. I notice the smell of dirt and animals and harvest: newness and life!

I lift my hands, put one over my chest. I pace my breath with the beat of my heart. Slow down, Mary, I tell myself. I lay the other across my abdomen, feel it rise and fall with each breath, deeper, fuller, rounder. Slow.

My soul magnifies the Lord. Breathe in. Wait. Breathe out.

My spirit rejoices in God my savior. A smile dances over my lips before I can even stop myself. I catch my breath. Breathe in. Wait. Breathe out.

I have just experienced the most incredible moment of my life – probably the most incredible moment of anyone's life that I know or will ever know.

As I am collecting water from the neighborhood well to take back to my father's home, an apparition stands before me. I am startled but I choke on my scream, too stunned to utter even a single sound. I realize my mouth is hanging open and I look around to see if anyone else is witnessing what is before me. Seeing no one, I splash cool water from the bucket to my face, blinking hard in disbelief. I used to hear these stories of angels – messengers from God – appearing to people for whom God had a special message but I didn't think that happened anymore. Those were just stories.

The messenger's voice is like thunder. "Greetings, you who are highly favored! The Lord is with you."

The Lord is with me? Why would an angel visit me, Mary of Nazareth, a girl with no special gifts, no social standing, no money, no education, no future? I am nobody. I am just a girl in a poor village. We are no one here. We try to stay hidden in plain sight.

> God has looked with favor on the lowliness
> of the Almighty's servant.

A year ago, I had become betrothed to a man who my father said would be a good and faithful husband. I was thirteen, the right age for a girl in my village to be pledged in marriage. Still, I was nervous and excited at the same time.

My mother had spent my whole life preparing me to be a wife: to care for a husband and the home and eventual children. She shuffled around the house, cooking and cleaning, muttering about how Adam may have been created first, but ever since God created Eve, women have been holding the whole world together. I folded barley and water together to make bread, giggling at her boldness, the last precious sounds of childlike joy slipping across my lips. Still, becoming someone's wife comes with the burden of responsibility. In this promise, I say farewell to girlhood and prepare for the expectations of womanhood.

Life in the village of Nazareth is simple. We are all alone here in the hills. Lots of people say nothing good ever comes out of Nazareth. We are a poor town with a bad reputation. In Rome's shadow, we are crushed by both religious laws and the empire. We are a community of struggling peasants. We keep our heads down, avoiding the Romans, just trying to get by on our own. We're a small village and we try to stay invisible. If we're invisible, maybe we'll be forgotten, and if we're forgotten, maybe trouble won't find us. We go to the Temple and offer our sacrifices. We pray. We obey. I dream of living in a world where we don't need to keep our eyes down, where we are not afraid, where we are free.

But who am I to wish for such things? I am just a girl. I will marry a man in the village. His name is Joseph, and even though we live in this small village, I don't know him well. My mother and father say that he is a kind man and that this is a good match. He is a hard worker from a hard-working family. It was as simple as that: we were betrothed to be married, and in a year, we would have our wedding ceremony. Joseph is a tradesman, a carpenter who works with his hands. Because of his trade, Joseph and his father spend lots of time outside of the city, working on projects for the Roman Empire.

I wonder if I will see him often. I wonder if I will miss him. I wonder if he will tell me about the wide world he sees outside of Nazareth. I wonder if he will ever take me away from here, and if he does, will I miss my family? I don't dream of a future in Nazareth, but this is where I was born, where I will raise children of my own, and where I will someday be buried.

Even more than these things, though, I wonder if I will learn to love Joseph as my cousin Elizabeth loves her husband Zechariah. I know I will move into Joseph's family's house soon, and that from now until the time of our wedding, Joseph will go to work building a room for us to raise our family in. In God's time, I will have children of my own and raise them, and sons will study the Scriptures with a teacher in the Temple and I will teach the girls to make bread and cheese, just as my mother did with me.

For better or for worse, I won't ever leave Nazareth and Nazareth won't ever leave me, not really. We will always be a part of each other. I wonder if there is anything left for me in Nazareth, what life is like beyond this little village, if God has any plans for us at all.

Perhaps these types of worries and questions are all the more reason for God to send a messenger to me, for all of my people, for just a time as this, for those of us who wish, deep down, for more for all of us, and better for our people.

This messenger from the Lord has a voice that is clear and mysterious, as demanding as thunder and as strong as the wind.

"Don't be afraid," he says.

I look around, in part to see if anyone else has noticed what I'm seeing, and in part to see if he's actually talking to me or to another. I look down at my feet, blistered from work, and I think of our ancestor Moses standing before God at Horeb. Am I supposed to take off my shoes? The question crosses my mind as quickly as a heartbeat.

"Mary," the voice interrupts my contemplation. I look up with a start. "I bring a message from the Lord. You will give birth to a son, and you are to give him the name Jesus. He will be great and will be called the Son of the Most High God. The Lord God will give him the throne of his father David, and he will reign over Jacob's descendants forever. God's kingdom will never end."

Excuse me? I feel my mouth gaping open, stuck, unable to speak. I look at the sky. It's a warm day but not hot. It's not that the heat has made me imagine this creature or this voice. I rub my eyes, thinking I am dreaming up this exchange, but the angel still stands there before me, bright, much cleaner than any man in all of Nazareth. I splash water over my face again, peering over the edge into the well. Maybe the water is bad.

"How..?" I try. I pause, remembering my mother telling me about Elizabeth's husband Zechariah, stricken mute and unable to speak after questioning the miraculous hand of God. I shift my eyes back to the angel, cautious. "How can this be true?" My voice shakes. "I have been with no man."

"The Holy Spirit will be with you, Mary," this messenger says. "The child you carry in your womb will be the Son of God. Trust the Lord in this: no word from God will ever fail."

Don't be afraid. Isn't that what this messenger of the Lord said? This has to be a joke, right? Don't be afraid when you are an unwed mother in the little town of Nazareth? Everyone knows Joseph and I are still months away from being married! I know what will happen to me. I'll be lucky if I get stares and sideways glances, if people tarnish my name and possibly even Joseph's. People will talk. They'll say we have no self-control. Or they'll gossip about my family. Or they'll speculate I was unfortunate enough to run into a Roman soldier on the road out of the village. Don't be afraid? Does this messenger from God not understand this news could cut me off from my family, banish me from my community, forbid me from the Temple? Don't be afraid? Doesn't God see me? Doesn't God care about me, about my future?

I know the reality I face if I am to accept this proposal: Joseph will end our betrothal, divorce me, and I will forever be an unmarried mother, as no righteous Jewish man would take a woman like me for a wife. My place will be with the widows: begging, hoping and relying on the generosity of others for my very survival. The worst case scenario, I know, is death by stoning for infidelity to Joseph. I will be shunned, excommunicated; I am just a peasant girl with no future and now my life will be over before it even begins.

I feel my heartbeat in my throat, in my ears, in my stomach. I can feel tears catch in the corners of my eyes. I never dreamed of a life in Nazareth, but this? I know my fate as a wife and mother – as a woman in Nazareth. This changes everything, though, and it is too much for me. I am too young to hand over my life.

I think about what else the angel said: The Lord God will give him the throne of his father David, and he will reign over Jacob's descendants forever. God's kingdom will never end.

Was this the Savior we had been looking for? The one we had been praying for all our lives, for generations? Could it be? We always imagined a King coming down in fiery victory over our enemies, riding on a chariot with a host of angels from above, not a child born to a nobody like me in a run-down, dirty, forgotten place like Nazareth. Who am I that the Lord should choose me to birth such a rescuer?

> The Mighty One has done great things for
> me – holy is his name.

I stare at my reflection in the bucket of water I am still cradling between my arms. My skin glows with sweat from my labor; dust and dirt are splotched across my face. This is what you look like when you live in a place like this. My hair, tucked hastily underneath my head covering, is peeking out from around my ears defiantly. I blink at myself. A single tear snags in my eyelashes. I never dreamed of a life in Nazareth. Dirty. Hiding. Forgotten. Or, at least, hoping to be forgotten. But I never dared to dream of anything different from Nazareth. Nobody thinks about living anywhere other than the place where they are.

> The Lord has been mindful of the humble
> state of his servant.

I think of all that it took to get us – my people – to this sleepy little town where we hope no one will find us, where we pay our taxes and pray that Caesar Augustus won't take our livestock and our land and will let us stay here in peace. It feels like my world is constantly upside-down, or about to be turned upside-down. I feel like I can never sit still, can never listen or wait. I feel like I have to be prepared for anything.

> He shows mercy to everyone, from one
> generation to the next, who honors him as
> God.

I think of the stories I've heard about what life is like in Jerusalem, the Holy City. I think of the stories of the wealthy people and the high priest who live in the Upper City. People who visit Jerusalem come back to Nazareth and tell extravagant stories about the marble villas and arched passageways, the walls and fortifications in the richest parts of the city.

But even more than that, I think of what our neighbors tell me about the poor people who live there, in Jerusalem's Lower City. The Lower City is so different from the Upper City. It has unpaved streets and simple limestone houses. The people there live their entire lives hidden in the shadows of great walls and columns. They are not unlike me and my family and the rest of the Nazarenes.

> He has brought down rulers from their thrones but has lifted up the humble.

The differences between those who live in the Upper City and those who are trying to survive in the Lower City are striking. The people are hungry there in the Lower City. They are dirty. They have only the clothes on their backs and their animals and each other. Like us in Nazareth, they are just trying to make a living, but unlike us in Nazareth, there is no hiding from Augustus and his soldiers who line the streets, and there is no praying to be invisible when the Temple priests come around.

> He has filled the hungry with good things but has sent the rich away empty.

God's kingdom will never end. God will remember and be merciful to Abraham and his descendants forever, just as he promised our ancestors.

I look up from my reflection. I look at the angel before me. I am scared. I am so scared. What will this mean for me? For Joseph? For our futures? But I remember the stories about the oppressed, the hungry. I remember our own oppression: crushed under both law and Caesar. I can imagine tired eyes. I remember the stories of our plight in Egypt, but because of oppression and injustice we are no more free now than we were then. I know the pain in my heart and I know the pain in the people. My people.

I know what I must do.

"I am the Lord's servant," I say with resolve. "May your word to me be fulfilled."

In this moment, I think of what this messenger told me about my cousin Elizabeth, and the voice that told her husband she will have a son named John in her old age. I think of Zechariah who had been made mute at the news of Elizabeth's pregnancy. We were all certain Elizabeth and Zechariah would never have children. I hold the news of what will soon become of me and I try to hold tight to this command: *do not be afraid.*

I breathe in. Wait. I breathe out. I think that the God who Rescues must be in the business of performing miracles.

REFLECTION GUIDE & QUESTIONS

- What happens to you when you feel overwhelmed? How do you typically react?

The angel Gabriel says to Mary, "Greetings, you who are highly favored." What do you think of when you consider the idea of being highly favored by God? Often we think of comfort and luxury and blessing. Instead, Mary faces explaining to her fiancé, and likely others, how she is pregnant. She'll have the scary responsibility of raising the son of God. And ultimately, though she doesn't know it, she'll face watching her son die on a cross. Yet knowing the path ahead will be difficult, and in the midst of a visit from an angel, which had to be overwhelming in itself, Mary responds to Gabriel by saying, "I am the Lord's servant. May your word to me be fulfilled."

- Do you wish God's favor for you was all comfort and luxury?
- How does Mary's story change how you understand God's favor?

We do not all venerate Mary in the same way, but we can note that no one, aside from Jesus, plays a more central role in the story of salvation than Mary. She faces public condemnation, gives up any social standing she may have had, and risks the great danger of childbirth in that time to fulfill God's plan. As she says yes to God, she finds a tremendous sense of peace and purpose in the promises of God.

- Are you ready and willing to surrender your life to God's leading as Mary does? Why or why not?
- What does it mean to "trust in the Lord with all your heart"?
- How is Mary an example and model of trusting God for you?
- What promises of God in Scripture can help you to trust?

CHAPTER 5

GOD WITH US
JOSEPH

Have you ever been angry? Of course you have. We all get angry sometimes. Have you ever been so angry you just wanted to break something? Or throw something? So angry you don't trust yourself in the moment? You've been there, huh? Me, too. Me, too.

I can recall in vivid detail the day I was that angry. Mary had just shared the news that she was with child, and I know that's supposed to be a happy moment for a young couple. But you've got to understand, we were betrothed, not yet married, and we'd never been intimate. When she told me she was going to have a baby, it was as though something inside me had broken. It was as if the life and the future I had hoped for, worked for, planned for, and prayed for had been ripped away from me. I was angry and sad and confused, all at the same time.

I don't know why that moment comes to mind now, except without that experience, this moment, this day, wouldn't be the same.

You see, there wasn't much to look forward to in Nazareth, which is why I was so excited about my marriage to Mary. Day after day, we men would work when there was work, tend the gardens when there wasn't work for hire, and hope to make ends meet. When there was work to be done, or should I say when the wealthy were paying for work to be done, we'd grab our tools and our mules and trek to Zippori, which the Romans call Sepphoris, just over an hour's walk from Nazareth. There we'd lay stonework or build their fancy homes. It would take us half a day to get there. Sometimes we'd be there for a week putting roofs on their expensive houses. We would sleep under the stars most nights, and sometimes when it stormed, they'd let us sleep in the frames of their unfinished homes. But sometimes not.

I remember a time I was working for a wealthy man in Zippori. One night, it was raining like mad, and, taking pity on us, he said if it got too wet we could go and sleep in his barn. I remember thinking to myself while preparing to sleep in that barn, "I never want to do this again."

Not that we complained too much about the circumstances, because there was money in the city and there was work. It could have been worse, you know. You'd leave those jobs and you'd feel so good about yourself because you'd have this satchel full of coins. But it was never as much as you thought it was. You'd have enough for food for a while, and maybe food for the animals, but not much more. Anything extra would end up in the hands of the tax collectors one way or another. The truth is, all we can hope for is a little work, and with occasional luck, a rich patron to take you on for a time and help you get ahead enough to get some land or a bigger home.

With so much insecurity in the world around us, our lives are built around family and the highlight of any life is a wedding. So, when Mary told me she was with child, I didn't hear anything else she said. I just saw my one real hope for joy in life disappearing. I was devastated, and I was angry.

Nazareth is a small place. There wouldn't be any hiding Mary's pregnancy. Everyone would know because everybody knows everybody, and everyone would have some opinion on the matter. There would be those who, if they found out the baby wasn't mine, would call for her to be stoned to death. That's part of our Jewish law, though I couldn't bear the thought of anyone dying, let alone while pregnant. That can't be right.

There would be others who would blame me, and shame me. I'd lose my honor in this community, and perhaps my employment possibilities, if people thought I was the father outside of marriage. Have you ever had a time when it seemed like no option was a good one? What choice did I have? Give up my one hope and dream in life? Give up my job? Give up my honor? Give up a life? None of these options seemed right.

I'm a faithful Jew. I follow the law. I try to orient my life toward God. I can't tell you how many times I asked, "Why me?" Have you ever asked that question? I don't know about you, but most often when I ask, I don't get an answer. Life doesn't suddenly become simple. Mary claimed she'd been visited by an angel. Could that be? Does that still happen? That's what I kept asking myself. Even if she was bearing the child of God, I thought, how can that be?

I was pretty sure God would not select a carpenter from Nazareth to be part of the royal family. Sure, my heritage traces back to King David, but those days are long past, and the family tree of David in my generation is too large to count. There are others with more standing, more influence. And none of these truths would change the fact that life would become impossible for us in a small town. I must admit now, I was leaning toward just breaking off the engagement quietly. I'd walk away, and Mary could maybe go somewhere with distant family where she could have the baby outside of the scorn of our community. To be honest, I didn't know what to do and I certainly didn't know what to believe anymore.

I went to bed a mess. Praying and thinking through every option, I was awake for so long. And then, finally, I fell asleep. And I dreamed. At least I think I dreamed. It seemed so real. A messenger of God appeared in the dream. I'm not sure how I knew he was a messenger. Something inside me just knew. And he said I shouldn't be afraid to take Mary as my wife, that indeed the child, just as Mary had said, was conceived by the Holy Spirit. Then the messenger spoke these words that touched my soul in a way I cannot put into words. He said, "you will call him Jesus, because he will save his people from their sins."

The name, Jesus, means "Yahweh saves." "God Saves." That's God's promise! The Torah, the Psalms, and the prophets all speak to this truth, this hope. God saves. God. Not us. God saves!

God has been silent for so long, but could it be? When we're young, we learn the words of the prophet Isaiah, who spoke of a young woman who will become pregnant and give birth to a son, and the Prophet says the name given to that child will be Immanuel. Immanuel means "God with us." God with us to save us. All of our Scriptures have these imperfect people – Noah, Abraham, Joseph, Jacob, and King David – and God moves the world through them. What if it's happening again? It couldn't be Mary and I, though, could it?

Was the dream real? When I woke up, I kept asking myself if it was real or not. I still couldn't believe it. Not really. It was too much.

Then I went from this sense of excitement and possibility to this feeling of just being overwhelmed. What if it was true? Me, raising a child that is God's? I can't do that. I'm not qualified. Surely God can't mean for me to do that. There are so many more questions than answers. Did all of this really happen? Why Mary? Why me? How can we do this? What will our families say? What will the people in town do and say? Can we get through this?

God saves. Since that day, right up to this one, I keep repeating the meaning of the name I was told to give the child. Jesus. God saves. Jesus. God saves. God is with us. God is with us. God is with us.

The day after my dream, I just kept repeating every word of the messenger. Over and over. Ultimately, I realized I had a choice. I'd always had a choice. In fact, we all have a choice, right? We can do our best to live in faith, following the signs God puts in our lives and believing God is with us and God saves. Or, we can choose to live without that truth, trying to make it on our own while living with no signs of God and taking everything as coincidence.

I have no idea what's going to happen. I have no idea what the future holds. I have no idea if Mary and I can do this, or even yet if it's real or just something in our imagination. But I am... actually we – Mary and I – are choosing faith. What do we have to lose in choosing to believe God is at work and can do things we can't fathom? We know God has shown God's truth through others in the past. Why not us? I know it sounds crazy, but I'm choosing faith. I'm choosing to believe the stories of God at work in unlikely ways through unlikely people are true. Wouldn't you?

I'm choosing to believe God saves. And I'm scared to death. Don't miss that part. I'm scared to death. But I'm trusting in the promise that God is with me. God is with us.

REFLECTION GUIDE & QUESTIONS

- Reflect on a time in your life when things didn't go according to plan. What happened? How did you feel at the time?

Consider what Joseph had to be thinking and feeling. In that time in the Jewish world, Joseph had two choices to deal with what he must have assumed was Mary's infidelity: he could publicly state his case against her, which could lead to Mary being stoned to death, or he could divorce her quietly. The Bible tells us Joseph was δικαιος (dikaios), a Greek word sometimes used for Jews who followed the Torah. It's really the opposite of sinful and implies someone is "just in the eyes of God," or does the right thing before God. The story then shares that Joseph gave thought about what to do.

- When you are making a big decision in life, how does your faith play a role?
- What are ways we can discern where God is leading us?

As Joseph is considering the right thing to do, he is visited in a dream. Imagine what he had to be thinking when he woke up. Was it real? If I do this, what will people say? Ultimately, Joseph decides to be faithful to God's word to him and to trust God. Notice the name he is to give the baby: Jesus. Names are almost always significant in the Bible. Jesus means "God saves," and Emmanuel means, "God with us." This is the promise Joseph will hold onto.

- Have you ever sensed God's presence in your life? If yes, share your experience.
- What spiritual practices (i.e. prayer, meditation, worship, serving others) most help you to know and sense God's presence?

CHAPTER 6

THE GIFT OF PEACE
AN INTERLUDE FROM GABRIEL

Most people, when they hear the word angel, picture flying beings all dressed in white, looking like they've been working out their whole lives, and glowing with halos around their heads. So, if you're wondering if I'm truly an angel, I am. I just look like a man. I should add, some of you always picture us naked from the waist up, or totally naked for that matter. I dressed today so you wouldn't worry about that.

I always find it kind of funny how human beings picture us so much from how fiction authors portray us, and less about what the Bible actually says about us. I see these old artworks of me with Mary, and in almost all of them I have wings and am floating. Yet in the book of Daniel, the Scriptures clearly convey that when I appear to humans, I look like a man. It's okay, though. In so many of those paintings, Mary always looks like a light-skinned European woman. I understand there are details to be filled in with any good story, details we often insert to better see ourselves in the narrative.

People have all kinds of ideas of what angels are and what we look like. And that's understandable. In the Bible, in the visions of Isaiah, Ezekiel, and Revelation, there are some wild images of the seraphim and cherubim – six wings, multiple heads. But you might notice that when we appear to humanity – Hagar, Gideon, Daniel, Zechariah, Mary, for example – we most often look like humans. You see, what's most important is that we are messengers of God. Literally, that's what we've been called. The Greek and Hebrew words first used to describe us mean exactly that: "messenger." We come to make known God's will, to make known what God is doing. Sometimes we come to help people know God's call in their lives. I came to help answer the prayer of Daniel who wanted to understand God's vision and what he was supposed to do with it. I came again to answer the prayer of Zechariah who prayed for forgiveness, deliverance, and for the messiah to come. You see, we angels stand in for the presence of God as messengers on God's behalf. Please don't worship us. Our whole existence is to point to God.

Which brings me to my encounter with Daniel. I remember when I first appeared to him. He was so afraid. He wrote that I looked like a man, and I did, but when you're in the presence of an angel, the sense of God's presence that we bring can be quite overwhelming. Daniel fell to the ground terrified. As I explained the vision to him, so he could see what God was doing, I gently lifted him back to his feet. I assured him I was here in answer to his prayer to understand the visions.

Zechariah was also gripped with fear when I appeared. I startled him by appearing right by the altar in the Temple. "Do not be afraid," I said to him. "Your prayer has been heard." Perhaps Zechariah was afraid of me or my appearance. Or maybe he was afraid of what God had to say. Or maybe he was just overwhelmed that God would choose to send an angel directly to him. Whatever the case, my role was to assure Zechariah, to help him believe, to see that he was going to play a part in God's story of grace and deliverance.

By the way, I want it on record: people sometimes say I took away Zechariah's voice, which wasn't very nice while his wife was pregnant. Please read that account again. As the story records, I didn't take away his voice. I, as a messenger, mind you, just delivered the message that he wouldn't be able to speak until the baby was born because he didn't believe my words. How the voice disappeared remains a mystery of God, but notice the experience led Zechariah to be a powerful witness of God's plans. Eventually.

Anyway, I should tell you about my encounter with Mary as well. Dear Mary. You know, when I appeared to Daniel, he was a servant in the King's court. When I appeared to Zechariah, he was an elder priest. Mary, though, was just beyond childhood when I visited her. She was a young woman about to play such a huge role in God's story. When I visited her, I said, "Greetings, you who are highly favored! The Lord is with you."

She wrinkled up her face, trying to comprehend what was happening, what I was saying. She seemed troubled, maybe afraid, I couldn't tell exactly. I could imagine the questions going through her mind. "Why me?" "I'm not a priest or a prophet, I'm just a peasant girl." "What does this mean?" "What is he going to say to me?"

I told her not to be afraid, my standard opening line. Then I shared the message: She would bear the son of God.

Now she was quite confused. "But how can this be?" she asked.

I explained the Holy Spirit would come upon her. That God's power would work this miracle. I told her about her relative Elizabeth. And then she surprised me.

You see, after I spoke to Daniel, he had remained fearful, exhausted by the visions and my appearance. After I spoke to Zechariah, he was still figuring out what it all meant. But Mary, dear Mary, she looked right at me. There was this look of determination in her eyes. Instead of being upset, she had this sense of peace surrounding her. And then she spoke these powerful words of faith: "I am the Lord's servant. May your word to me be fulfilled."

"I am the Lord's servant. May your word to me be fulfilled." Mary paused and pondered her own words for a moment, and then seemed to find a peace in saying yes to God's call in her life.

God's call, the visions God gives through the Holy Spirit, aren't always easy to hear or accept. In fact, sometimes they seem impossible. But when we angels say, "Don't be afraid," we say it with an invitation to find peace that God is active and at work in your life. We invite humans to find peace by accepting God's call without fear, by trusting in God's power.

So often you humans think you don't have a role to play. You think your faith isn't strong enough. Or you aren't gifted enough. Or you aren't qualified enough or faithful enough to serve like your pastor or your faith mentor. The thing is: that just isn't true. God has a role for you – for everyone – to play. We angels are tasked with assuring you, especially you, have a role to play in God's story.

You see, peace comes from living with the assurance of God's deliverance. Peace comes in answering God's call instead of denying it or running from it. Humans think so often that peace comes from shows of power, or domination, or knowing everything, or everything in life being perfect. "We'll find peace by destroying the enemy," you think. "We'll find peace if we get rid of all the problems," you say. "We'll find peace if we have enough that we don't have to worry," you imagine. And you continue to search for peace in all of these places unsuccessfully.

Mary found it. Peace, I mean. The peace she would need to weather the critique of family and community. The peace she would need to raise the child of God. The peace she would need to watch him die on a cross. She found this peace in a few simple words in answer to God's invitation to be a part of the story. "I am the Lord's servant. May your word to me be fulfilled."

"Peace on earth, goodwill to all humanity." After Mary gave birth, I joined in this chorus of the angels to celebrate that which God had promised was coming to be. I helped invite the shepherds, those who felt most removed from society's loops of influence, to be the first to visit this baby who would change everything.

Peace on earth. That's my prayer, our prayer for humanity. May you find peace in answering God's call; peace in knowing God invites you to be part of a story of love and grace; peace in the assurance of God's promises made real in Jesus.

REFLECTION GUIDE & QUESTIONS

- Reflect on when you feel most at peace.

The angel Gabriel's first appearance in the Bible is not in the New Testament. He first appears in the book of Daniel, where his role is to explain the visions Daniel is experiencing. Daniel says Gabriel looked like a man, and as he approached, Daniel was terrified. Later, Daniel says Gabriel "came to me in swift flight" (NIV).

- What images come to mind when you think of angels?
- Which of these images do you think are in the Bible?
- What roles do angels serve in the Bible?

The words for angel in Hebrew and Greek both mean messenger. Hebrews 1:14 says, "Are not all angels ministering spirits sent to serve those who will inherit salvation?" Angels serve God by sharing God's message with faithful servants – Abraham, Daniel, Zechariah, and Mary, for example. Often, the angel's message is to not be afraid, and then to hear and trust God's call.

- Why do you think the Bible uses the phrase, "do not be afraid" 81 times (in the NIV translation)?
- How do you find peace and assurance in God's promises?
- What does the peace of Christ look like in the everyday lives of followers of Jesus?
- How do you believe God sends messages of peace today?
- What is one way you can seek and experience God's peace?

CHAPTER 7

A PROMISE
A SHEPHERD

I remember the day I knew I'd be a shepherd my whole life. My brother and I were arguing. We'd already been in trouble that day with dad for chasing a sheep around for fun, and now, even in imagination games, we were competing with each other.

"I'm a nobleman, and you're just a shepherd that works for me," my brother had declared as he wanted us to continue playing his way.

"Oh yeah," I answered, "well I'm a mighty warrior who is more famous than your nobleman."

"I'm the general that commands the army and you," my brother said.

"I'm the king that commands the general," I replied.

"Well I'm the emperor who now rules the world!" he said.

At that moment my dad put his hand on my shoulder. I didn't even know he was coming up behind me. He turned me around to face him and he said, "Son, I know you have dreams from all of the stories you've grown up with, but you're a young man now. We're shepherds. You are going to be a shepherd." Suddenly what was a game with my brother became a teaching moment for my dad.

"David became a king," I told him with a little rebellion in my voice, not wanting my dream of a life beyond the fields to disintegrate.

"David was chosen by God to be King," my dad said. "Our role is here. We're shepherds."

"Well, I'm going to be so good that someone will gift me some sheep of my own. Or maybe I'll just go and build things for the king, like the Herodion. Someday I'm going to move into Bethlehem and have my own home, not just a tent, and I'm going to pay a shepherd to watch my sheep."

The truth was, I didn't want to be in the fields my whole life with just enough to live on, and my dad seemed to be saying that wasn't possible. I knew he was right. In this world, if you're the son of a shepherd, you can't read or write, you aren't educated, and the only thing you truly know how to do is care for the animals. If you want to make a living you do the only thing you know: care for sheep and goats. Well, care for the sheep and goats of others.

About two months later, my dad presented me with a crook and said it was time I begin taking a night shift with him. He told me what an honorable profession shepherding was. "We take care of the animals that provide food and milk and sustenance for the whole area," he said. "And even more important, we take special care of the animals that will be sacrificed to God as gift offerings at the Temple. This is holy work we do."

"Whatever, Dad." That was my only response.

That was 25 years ago. Twenty-five years; it's hard to believe. And now, here I am, one of the elders of our family of shepherds. My dad was right, of course.

He's gone now, my dad. I miss him.

Sheep herding is hard work and it takes a toll. If you don't know that, you probably haven't tried to get a sheep or goat to do what you want instead of what the animal has in mind. We're out in the elements all the time, living on the land, dealing with the threat of wild animals and thieves. My dad was just worn down in the end. He did his best to provide for us, and it meant long, hard years of work.

I remember my dad used to tell us this joke all the time. "What's the difference between a shepherd and a king? The shepherd has a crook and the king is one." I stopped laughing when I was a kid because he told it so often, but now I share the joke with others and I get it. What little we have is taxed to keep us from ever having more.

Sometimes I feel like I'm just going through the motions of life. We get up with the sun. We take the herd out into the hills to find a fresh place to graze and feed. We chase the straggler. We search for the wanderer. We scrounge up whatever we can to eat for lunch. We watch. We sit and try to stay cool in the hot sun. We return the herd to safety for the night. We eat dinner. We set the night watch for wild animals or thieves. We get up tomorrow and repeat. Life spins along.

I have to tell you, I'm a 40-year-old shepherd. I stop sometimes and think, "Does my life really matter? What difference have I made?" The truth is, when I'm gone, nobody is going to miss that shepherd they passed by on the road. The owners of our flock will find another shepherd, perhaps not as honest or trustworthy, but they won't care as long as they're making money. How can one person's simple life have any meaning?

My family says I think too much about it, that there is joy in family and work well done. I suppose so. But I've grown tired of being dirty all the time. I've grown tired of being shunned by most people because we can't get to Temple and we don't practice the Sabbath because someone has to watch the animals. I've grown tired of never having enough money or possessions to do more than feed my family. I've begun to think maybe my dad was right. I'm just a shepherd, and I'll always be just a shepherd. As of a few days ago, all of the joy had been sucked out of life for me. I was just going through the motions.

And then... and then!

Look, I know people are going to think we're crazy. They're going to say we shepherds have been out there away from people for so long that we're seeing things or making things up. But this was real.

This person, or being (words can't fully describe it), was real. This person appeared in the field just beyond the pen we'd created for the herd and there was this glow all around. It's not like anything I'd ever seen before. It just glowed. Everywhere. We fell to our knees, not sure what to think or what was going to happen next. And this person, this being, was real, but not real. I know it all sounds made-up but I pinched myself several times. This was not a dream. Several of us shepherds were witnesses. And the being spoke.

And the first words he said were, "Don't be afraid."

"TOO LATE!"

That's the first thing that went through my head. Of all the possibilities in that moment, in the presence of some mystical being, all I could think was, "too late, I'm already afraid." How could I not be afraid when some being just appears and shines like the stars and then starts speaking? We were afraid, alright.

To be honest, none of us could remember everything the messenger said. Between us, we had to piece together the details because just as the messenger finished, the sky lit up and the voices seemed to come from every direction around us, singing this song. Oh, the song...

Yes, the song. The voices sang of glory to God and of peace. They were so beautiful. I just wanted to stay in that minute of my life forever and ever. And maybe that sounds crazy, but it was a crazy kind of night. You could see it in the eyes of those around me – my sister, my brother, the other shepherds. This moment wasn't like anything we had ever experienced. Nothing else mattered. Profound joy hung in the air like nothing I've ever known. When the song ended and the skies cleared, we all just stood in silence. I honestly think everyone felt like I did. Sad, sort of. Like I'd witnessed something that was now gone and that I wished would have lasted forever.

After a few minutes, we began looking at each other. We all carried that sort of dumb, sort of questioning, "I hope I'm not the only one who saw and heard that" kind of look. But we all saw and heard the same things. We pieced together the message of the angel, who'd said our savior would be born in Bethlehem. And then he said to look for a baby wrapped and lying in a manger, which seemed kind of odd. Christ, the Messiah, the savior of the world, laying in a manger. It didn't make much sense, but after that experience, we sure wanted to see what came next. We quickly found someone to watch the sheep and we headed over the hill road and into Bethlehem. It wasn't a long walk to begin with, but we made it in record time.

When we arrived and asked around, we found that, sure enough, a couple had arrived in town and for some reason no family took them in. They ended up in the stable of one of the larger homes, so we went there. We entered the stable cautiously and were welcomed by this quiet man who asked what brought us to his family that night. We told him and the young mother the whole story. The mother just smiled and listened and seemed to take in every word. And then I looked at the baby. To be honest, I'm not sure why I didn't look at him as soon as we arrived, but for some reason it took me a moment to take in the whole scene. I looked, and there was the baby just as the messenger had said. I fell to my knees.

When a firstborn lamb is delivered, one of the tasks of the shepherd is to examine it for blemishes. To be offered in sacrifice at the Temple, one of the requirements of the law is that it be perfect. I don't know if you've tried to corral a baby lamb and examine it, but it isn't a particularly easy task. One of the best ways to both examine and protect it is to wrap it up in cloth and lay it somewhere snug, like a manger. Here was the savior of the world, wrapped and lying in a manger. The savior of the world, that's what the messenger said. The savior of the world. Our savior.

God chose us. Us. Nobody ever chooses shepherds for anything, but God chose us to share in this news. God chose me. Which makes me think of my dad. "Shepherding is an honorable profession," he told me. This is holy work. Holy work.

I don't know how to describe this joy. I have this place in God's story. Kind of like David, I guess. I'll go back to tending sheep now. It's what I know. And the world will continue to shun and ignore us unclean strangers in the field. But it will never be the same. This world is changing. And I have the joy of knowing, knowing this Messiah has come for me, for everyone. I have the joy of telling others.

REFLECTION GUIDE & QUESTIONS

- Tell about a time when something good happened to you that you didn't expect. Or share a gift you've received that was a true surprise.

The Gospel of Luke reveals Jesus as the savior of all, Jews and Gentiles, and was sent with a mission to the poor, the excluded, and the sinner. From the very beginning of Luke's account of Jesus' life, these themes emerge as He is born of a peasant girl in an unheard-of small place, and His first visitors are not people of power or influence but shepherds tending their flocks at night. We're invited to imagine what the shepherds must have thought and experienced as angels appear and invite them to visit this Christ child.

- What is the most joy you have ever felt?
- What's the most terrified you've ever been?
- How do you think these experiences would compare to seeing the skies filled with angels praising God and inviting you to meet the Messiah?

Have you ever been invited to a party where you felt underdressed? Or have you ever been in the presence of powerful people and felt a little overwhelmed? Or have you received something and felt unworthy? Perhaps the shepherds wondered why they were chosen by God that night, but as they visited the child they were caught up in the majesty and wonder of meeting Jesus, "glorifying and praising God" for all they witnessed.

- How would you share your experience of the Good News of Jesus with someone else?
- How has knowing Jesus impacted your life?
- How can you reach out this week with a word of support to someone you know who may feel disconnected, excluded, or may be going through a difficult time?

CHAPTER 8

MAKING ROOM
THE INNKEEPER

(If you read through the Biblical account, you'll find that despite the prominent role of the innkeeper in most children's Christmas pageants, there is no mention of an innkeeper in the Biblical story. What might we discover, though, if we imagine searching for a room that night in Bethlehem?)

Hello. And welcome to Bethlehem. As an innkeeper here in our village, it's a joy to greet you and tell you how wonderful it is to have you with us. We are proud of our community. Perhaps you know that the matriarch of Jewish heritage, Rachel, Joseph's mother, is buried here. In addition to that, we are the home of King David, and where he was anointed king. We're not a capital or a big city and place of power like Jerusalem, but our roots are deep. Did you know that Bethlehem means "house of bread" in the language of the Jews, and "house of meat" or "house of blood" in Arabic? Here in the hills, not far from Jerusalem, our community provides grain and meat for the region, and animals, lambs in fact, for the Temple sacrifice. We have an important place in the story of this land and this people.

You chose a busy time to visit. The census has brought a lot of people with ancestral roots here. We all know the census is just the Roman Empire's way of collecting our money, and making sure that we know we're controlled by them. They want us to know Caesar is in charge. I guess I shouldn't complain. As one with a spare room or two to share, it's a good time for innkeepers.

While you're here you might want to visit the Herodion. Most folks are sure King Herod is a bit of a maniac, obsessed by his desire for power and wealth and showing everyone how great he is. That, and he seems to kill off any family member who threatens him. But the guy sure can build. He had slaves and workers move land to create the highest mountain in the Judean wilderness, and then he built a palace on top of it – the Herodion. It's a bit of a hike, but a sight to see, I tell you. It will give you an idea of the kind of wealth and power Herod has in comparison to our poor town.

Well, good luck finding a place to stay. I recommend you track down a cousin or distant family member. That's your best bet.

You've tried already, you say? That's why you're still here.

Perhaps you heard we squeezed one more family in for the night just a bit ago, but those were special circumstances. A couple arrived from Nazareth. Four days of rugged travel. I don't know where you came from, but those roads can be rough, and to add to it, the young woman was pregnant. Like, very pregnant.

The man's family had ancestral roots here, and I'm not sure why their immediate family wouldn't create a little space for them. For whatever reason, they were needing a place and she knew the baby was coming. I am distantly related, and I couldn't very well turn them away. But we're packed with more people than we ever imagined, so I found them some room in our stable area. Don't think barn. People make that mistake. Rich people have barns. Our animals come in for the night to keep them safe and stay in what is essentially a room to the very back of the house, carved into the rock back there. I just moved the animals into one end and tried to clean up a little area as best I could. Not perfect, but a safe and warm place for the night.

This couple, undoubtedly stressed, had a sense of urgency knowing this baby was coming and they needed a place to stay. There was something about them, though. I don't know the word. Confidence? Sort of resolute? They just seemed to trust that everything would be okay. They weren't afraid. In fact, as I was trying to think how we could help them, I heard them each say that God would see them through this. Faith! That's what they had. Faith that somehow it would be okay.

Have you ever had a list of things you want, and maybe you've even received some of the things on that list of wants, but they didn't really make a lasting impact in your life? And then you received a gift you didn't expect, something you needed but you didn't even know you needed. Only now that you've received it, your life will never be the same. That's exactly what happened to us.

My wife and I, when we decided to use our extra room as a guest room and create a little inn for travelers on these roads, hoped for a little more income. We wanted a little more security in life, maybe even a luxury or two over time, a bed instead of our mats, some good oil, a new sheep or goat or two. When the census was called, nobody was happy about it, but the influx of people would be good for us; good for making a little more. And don't get me wrong, more visitors and more money has been good, though with taxes and the growing influence of the Roman Empire, our lives aren't so different.

I've realized now, more money and more luxury is what we wanted, what we thought would change things. But they didn't, and as it turns out, they weren't what we needed.

The young couple – Mary and Joseph – they had the baby. I mean, I guess I should say, she had the baby. My wife and a couple of women helped with the birth. They took the child when it was born and wrapped him up tight and laid him in a manger. Everyone said how cute and adorable he was. I've always thought babies when first born were a little strange-looking, but I kept my mouth shut. It was a joy to see how happy Mary and Joseph were.

I have to tell you, though, about what happened next. These shepherds arrived at my home, right out of the field. You could smell them coming. Without considering how I might react, they came straight in and said they had to see the baby that was born. I asked them how they knew, and they said a messenger of God came to the fields and told them the savior of the world, the Messiah, had been born in Bethlehem.

"Here?" I pondered, looking at them and trying to tell if they were serious. Or if they were crazy.

At that moment, hearing the commotion, Joseph came into the room and said it was okay. They could come back to see the baby.

Look, I'm not necessarily proud of this, but I stood just outside the door and listened to the conversation. The shepherds again recounted how a messenger had shared the news and then was joined by a singing army. Mary and Joseph just listened. They weren't surprised in the least bit. Then they recounted how they had each been visited by a messenger and told the same, and how the baby's name would be Jesus, Emmanuel, God with us.

Do you remember how I said Bethlehem has deep roots? There are these Scriptures in the prophets of old, of Micah and Isaiah, and most of the Jews here in Bethlehem know them by heart. They say:

> "But you, Bethlehem Ephrathah,
>   though you are small among the clans of Judah,
>   out of you will come for me
>   one who will be ruler over Israel,
>   whose origins are from of old,
>   from ancient times."

And then they go on:

> "Therefore, the Lord will give you a sign.
>   The young woman is pregnant and is about to give
>   birth to a son, and she will name him Immanuel"
>   There will be vast authority and endless peace
>   for David's throne and for his kingdom,
>   establishing and sustaining it
>   with justice and righteousness
>   now and forever."

Do you see? Do you understand? This child. What they are saying is that this is the child who will rule, who will usher in this kingdom of God that we've hoped for.

My heart is warmed tonight in a way I've never experienced. If this is God's child, everything is changing from here forward. A kingdom is about to begin, of peace and hope. That's what God has promised. I don't need more money or status to be secure. I need to know God's promise is real.

I know, somehow, in this birth of a child in my stable, God's promise is real.

Faith. I can't explain why I believe the story of this couple and these shepherds. Maybe because this child is the gift I didn't even know I needed. Maybe because I don't have anything to lose by putting my faith in this baby Jesus. If the promise is real, and I believe it is, my life will be saved by this child.

I'm so glad I made room. I hope you will as well. In your hearts and lives, I mean. To celebrate this birth as a gift, we just need to make room in our hearts and lives for Jesus.

REFLECTION GUIDE & QUESTIONS

- What is something that became a blessing that you didn't even know you wanted or needed?

Luke's account of the birth of Jesus begins with several important notes, including the census called by Caesar Augustus and the governorship of Quirinius. In contrast to the powers of the world at the time, the birth of Jesus takes place in a stable.

- How does the kingdom Jesus will bring differ from the kingdoms of then and now?
- What does having faith in Jesus mean to you?

While there isn't an innkeeper in Luke's account of the birth of Jesus, the story does say that there wasn't a "guest room" available. This could mean that the inns were full. It could also mean that none of Joseph's family would "make room" for the couple knowing Mary was pregnant outside of wedlock, but provided somewhere "away" from the family, like a stable in the back.

- What do you think Mary and Joseph were feeling as they searched for a place to have the baby?
- In what ways do we crowd Jesus out of our lives?
- What do you need to do to make room in your life for Jesus?

CHAPTER 9

GOOD NEWS
Simeon and Anna

"Most people don't actually know who we are. I'm Anna, and this is Simeon. We're just regular people, really. We're unremarkable in every possible way. We're not community leaders; we haven't had any great achievements; and we haven't done anything that make people famous. We've simply spent our entire lives around the Temple, serving and waiting."

"You're almost right, Anna. I am not remarkable, but I wouldn't say the same about you. I've come to know Anna over my years of visiting the Temple. She is always here. And by always, I mean day and night you'll find her in the outer courtyard praying and worshiping. The Temple regulars say she's been here every day since she lost her husband after only eight years together. And that was more than fifty years ago. How old are you, Anna? I'll tell you this. Women aren't allowed into the inner courtyard, but if they were, Anna might be the first they let in. I don't know a more devout and dedicated woman."

"You flatter me, Simeon. I am simply dedicated to serving my Lord, and the Temple is where I tend to see the evidence of the love and grace I'm looking for. It's hard to be a widow, especially when you become one when you're so young! Simeon here is a quite righteous and pious man himself, though. He won't tell you that: he's too humble. But let's just say this good man has a direct line to the Holy Spirit. Tell them, Simeon, about our experience together."

"To understand the whole story, I should probably start at the beginning. I was raised in a good Jewish family and taught that the Temple is the center of our lives. Here, we encounter God's presence. But even life around the Temple hasn't been the same since the Romans came to power here. Dishonest money changers. Tax collectors. Every day it feels like the corrupt power of the empire and the greed of this world infringes closer and closer to the Holy of Holies. Life outside of the Temple has grown even worse. The religious leaders have an agreement with Rome, but that doesn't mean life is easy for the rest of us, the people of God. No one is free of the reach of Caesar. That's what people say. And it's true.

"When we were little, Anna and I both were taught that a messiah, a deliverer, would come, and that God's kingdom would be restored. I waited my entire life holding onto that promise. I must admit, as I grew old, I began to wonder if I would see it. Then one day I was in the Temple courtyard praying, and I'm not sure how to describe what happened next. I've tried to share that I heard a voice, and people ask if it was in my head. It wasn't, I'm sure of it. I've tried to describe how I felt a presence, but people have asked me to explain it, and I can't. What I know is that I received a very clear message, that I would not die before I had seen the Lord's Messiah. And I don't know how to tell you how I knew it wasn't a dream or a hallucination. I just felt this incredible peace, this sense that I knew it was true. The Holy Scriptures speak of the Spirit of the Lord moving the judges of old

to follow God's instructions. That's the best way I can describe what I experienced. The Spirit of the Lord gave me this assurance. For days that turned into weeks that turned into months I held onto this promise.

"I felt like time standing still. I waited and waited, fearful I might miss the messiah, or maybe I had just made it up. But when I told people about it, that sense of peace would wash over me again, and those who didn't think I was crazy found some hope in what I was saying. So, I held onto that hope. And then, that day came, the day when my path crossed with Anna's in a way that changed everything."

"I will always remember that day, Simeon. Mary and Joseph arrived in the Temple courtyard with two small birds. Everyone knew what was happening when a couple came to the Temple with a baby and two small birds, or maybe a goat for that matter. It was consecration day, which is the day of presenting a sacrifice for the first-born child. The Law says every firstborn male is to be consecrated to the Lord. New parents were always especially nervous, wondering if they were doing things right. The two birds were a quick giveaway. Two birds were the substitute offering for a goat, and meant they were poor. Most couples are poor. That's just the reality we live in. Only a handful of the religious leaders' families have enough to bring a goat for a sacrifice. So, when Mary and Joseph walked into the Temple courtyard, everyone looked their way and knew why they were coming to the Temple. And that was when I saw Simeon come bounding across the courtyard. Simeon, you looked like you were a young man again: you shot across the courtyard so fast!"

"I knew, Anna. I just knew. That day I'd been walking down a street in Jerusalem and I had the same experience of the Spirit speaking to me as I did the day I was assured I would see the

Lord's Messiah. 'Now! Today,' I heard clearly. I knew this would be the day. So, I headed to the Temple courts, and when I saw that couple come in, I just knew. I can't tell you how I knew. I just knew. This was the Messiah. I went and held the baby in my arms and God's word just flooded into me. I gave thanks for this gift I was receiving from God. God's promise was fulfilled. My life was now complete. There was nothing else I wanted from life more than this moment. I couldn't help but say out loud the hymn I was carrying in my heart:

> For my eyes have seen your salvation,
> which you have prepared in the sight of all nations:
> a light for revelation to the Gentiles,
> and the glory of your people Israel.

"Then I turned to Mary. Here was this young woman, barely beyond a girl, and there was no way for her to fully know what this meant. This was God's promise coming to being, but there would be political shockwaves from this news. There would be those who hated this child, who wanted this child dead. There would also be those who would flock to this baby and put their hope in him. She needed to know what the future would hold, how difficult it may be. So, I told her the truth. 'A sword will pierce your own soul, too.' She looked at me with knowledge beyond her years, with a faith that gave me hope. And then Anna walked up."

"I had to, didn't I? You were going to scare that poor couple to death, especially a new mother with a fresh baby! I had been at the Temple every day for years, praying and worshiping and trusting in God's presence. God had shown me much in all that time. As I fasted, I came to trust God. As I prayed, I saw God's faithful hand at work across generations. I saw the sin and the struggle that would lie ahead from the religious leaders' cozy relationship with

Rome and the ways they have abandoned their people. So when that couple walked in, and I saw you running toward them, I also knew. I also can't tell you for certain how I knew, but I did, somehow. I could feel the confidence rise up in my chest, could feel my heart quicken with certainty.

"Even in that moment, I knew this would be the day everything would change. I felt a hope in my heart like an answered prayer. It felt like it took forever to get to you, like I was racing against time. When I reached you, I saw that same look of joy and wisdom in Mary's eye. Reflected in her, I saw peace and hope in the life of that newborn baby, and I gave thanks to God. And then I realized, this is news worth sharing. For everyone who has been waiting for deliverance, for those long-suffering, for those wondering if God will ever show up, for those at the edge and on the margins of a changing world that seems to be leaving them behind: we needed to let them know. So I started telling them. Everyone who was hoping for redemption of Jerusalem – for the kind of community that God showed God's people in the Holy Scripture – I told them it was arriving. As unbelievable as it seemed, this baby would bring this kingdom into being and would show us the way. We all thought the messiah would be a king, but God surprised us with a baby instead, born to a poor couple in a forgotten village. It sounds ridiculous but I knew it to be true."

"You know, Anna, we won't see that day ourselves. We're both too old."

"I'm not so sure I agree, Simeon. What does it mean to see that day? In the presence of that baby, you said you felt your life was complete. That was it: God's promise fulfilled. I felt the same thing. God's kingdom will be fully restored some day, of that I am certain. For us, the gift is being a part of it, of being able to share in it, of being able to experience it and talk about it with others. We get to be part of this story, part of announcing to the world that God is here, that God hasn't abandoned us. We get to point out to those who can't see it – or who think they can't keep waiting – that the waiting is worth it, that God is present. This is our day. God's kingdom is here right now and is also coming. We just have to claim it and share what we have seen."

REFLECTION GUIDE & QUESTIONS

- When have you waited and waited, knowing the wait would be worth it in the end?

Most people know the stories of Mary and Joseph, the shepherds, and the wise men from the Bible, but fewer know about Simeon and Anna. Because their story falls after Christmas, sermons about the two of them are rare. Simeon, according to Luke's Gospel, is a devout man who is prompted by the Holy Spirit to know he would see the Messiah before he died.

- How can looking forward to something impact how you live day to day?
- Have you ever felt prompted by the Holy Spirit to do something or say something? If yes, did you do it, and what happened?

Anna, according to Luke, spent more than 50 years faithfully praying day after day in the Temple. Her story is told in only three verses, yet she becomes the first person after the birth story to begin telling people about Jesus.

- What does it mean to you to be part of God's story?
- How can you share what you've seen God doing in your life or in the life of others?

CHAPTER 10

THE STORY DOESN'T BEGIN HERE
A WISE MAN

Wise people know their story is part of a much wider, much grander story, and find both comfort in this truth and an invitation to see themselves as part of the greater story.

Some call us magi, or wise men. We're from the east, or you might say where the sun rises. We're advisors to the kings and rulers of the Persian Empire. Some might call us priests or prophets. We study and we listen, and we look at the signs in the stars. Sometimes when we have a sense of what is happening in the world, we advise kings and rulers on how to respond. Not long ago, as we were studying the stars, we noticed a super bright star, like nothing we'd ever seen before. It was in the sky to the west, and it was aligned in the constellations in a configuration we attributed to the Kingdom of Israel. We believed the star might lead us there. In fact, the star, so bright, would likely be an indication that a great king had been born there.

There was once a wise man named Daniel who was exiled to Persia from Judah and became part of the team of advisors to our kings. As soon as I saw the star, I remembered a line in one of the scrolls Daniel brought that is still in our library. I looked it up and found these verses:

> "Then he spoke his message:
> 'The prophecy of Balaam son of Beor,
> the prophecy of one whose eye sees clearly,
> the prophecy of one who hears the words of God,
> who has knowledge from the Most High,
> who sees a vision from the Almighty,
> who falls prostrate, and whose eyes are opened:
> I see him, but not now;
> I behold him, but not near.
> A star will come out of Jacob;
> a scepter will rise out of Israel...'"

In this story, God had used a non-Hebrew prophet to speak to God's people of a coming king who would deliver them. What if this star of Jacob we were seeing in the sky was a sign of a coming king once again? We had to see for ourselves.

The journey would not be easy. A few hundred years ago, the Persian king Darius the Great built a highway for trade and communication to facilitate the growth of the empire. The road has remained open for years, and provides some security and ease of travel, but one still must worry about thieves along the way, and soldiers at checkpoints who demand a little extra for the "security" they provide. Safety has a cost. This royal road of Darius leads to the King's Highway, an even more ancient road, to complete the journey to the land of Jacob. The entire journey would be three to four months, traveling mostly by foot day after day, resting during the heat and pressing on into the night when visibility for travel allows.

Knowing the danger, we set out to follow the star to the west, traveling the known roads. We packed gifts to share along the way, loading camels and horses with supplies and food. Days turned into weeks, and weeks into months, the star to the west always there, leading us by night. Finally, we arrived in the land of Jacob.

Honestly, we weren't sure what to do next. No one we talked to along the road seemed to know anything was happening, so we veered off a bit from the star and went to Jerusalem. We figured if new royalty was coming into the world, the most likely place would be there in the capital of the region.

Have you ever been on a treasure hunt? That's kind of what this felt like, only when we arrived in Jerusalem we didn't find a new king being born, so we asked King Herod what he might know, and he seemed kind of disturbed. He ordered his advisors to consult, and they recalled a Scripture from their holy books that said a ruler would come from Bethlehem. We headed there with his blessing, though he continued acting strangely from the time he first heard our news of a great king being born. I didn't trust him.

When we arrived in Bethlehem, the star led us to this smaller place where a few people heard a child had been born. We knocked and were allowed in, and there was the child.

The child who will be a king. Born not in a palace but in a stable. None of us had the words to describe this moment.

The scrolls say "The people who walk in darkness will see a great light; Those who live in a dark land, the light will shine on them." This indescribable sense of light coming into the world might be the best way I can describe it.

So, that's how we arrived in Bethlehem, how we met the anointed child. We were overjoyed. Have you ever been so happy you're not even sure how to describe the feeling? That's how we feel. It's beyond words. And as we bowed before that child and laid our gifts – gold and frankincense and myrrh - at his feet, I kept thinking how this moment could change the world.

To understand how we feel, you need to know this isn't the beginning of the story. There's so much more.

Do you remember that wise man named Daniel who was in Persia with our ancestors? He left us these stories of the one true God. This God created human beings in God's own image. All of us. And then God gave them the ability to choose to love. And this God, even when people turned away, loved them and sent prophets to show them the way. This God forgave them, over and over. And the prophets promised that, eventually, God would send a messiah - a chosen one - who would bring peace and an everlasting kingdom of love and goodness. Daniel was willing to stake his life on this God and this God's promises.

Our world today truly needs this promise. Kings do battle. The rich take advantage of the poor. People suffer from illness and are cast out when they are suffering. Innocent people die. Rulers like Herod abuse their power, building great monuments to themselves with little thought for those who suffer. We need hope for a better future, a way forward with love in the midst of the grief and greed of the world. Daniel and the other prophets of whom he taught showed us this hope in God's promises. That's what brought us to this child. To this place.

There's this writing from Daniel. He had a vision of this future king, and this is what he wrote in the scrolls we have:

> "I saw one like a human being
> coming with the clouds of heaven.
> And he came to the Ancient One
> and was presented before him.
> To him was given dominion

and glory and kingship,
that all peoples, nations, and languages
should serve him.
His dominion is an everlasting dominion
that shall not pass away,
and his kingship is one
that shall never be destroyed."

This baby, this child, if the promises and signs are true, is God in human form, the Messiah coming to usher in this kingdom of peace and love as Daniel spoke of. Here we are, in this unremarkable home away from the lure of power and wealth, with this incredible young woman who gave birth and talks about her experience with such faith and joy, with this man who seems so humble and kind, in the presence of this child that leaves us feeling overwhelmed with joy in a way that I can't describe. I believe the promise. I believe this child is the Messiah, and that he will grow up and change the world.

Hope. That's what I feel in the presence of this child. Hope that the promise is true. Hope that this isn't the end of the story, but part of a much greater story, of which I am privileged to a small part.

REFLECTION GUIDE & QUESTIONS

- Share what you know about your family history. Where does your story begin?

Some scholars believe the wise men, or magi, likely came from Persia, which is modern day Iraq. If this is true, it is possible they would have known of Daniel, a Jewish prophet who in the exile became an advisor (wise man) in the king's court in Babylon in the Persian Empire. Daniel may have recorded and passed down Jewish teaching and the Torah (the first five books of the Bible) and his own visions of kingdoms rising and falling. If so, such teaching and knowledge of the prophets would have helped the wise men see in the stars the sign of a great king to be born in the land of Jacob.

If the wise men knew of this text and others that predicted the coming of a messiah, a chosen one of God, then they traveled west to meet a king unlike any other.

- Think of a time when you had great expectations about something coming up in the future. Did the event live up to the expectations? Why or why not?

The story the wise men travel into is a story that begins with God's creation of humanity and continues with God reaching again and again into the lives of humankind to show God's love and grace, but it is also a story of humankind continually turning away.

The wise men have studied a world of rulers coming and going, of war and strife, of humanity separated from God. They travel to encounter a king like no other. If what the prophets spoke is true, this child to whom they bow down and worship will change the world and usher in a new kingdom unlike any other.

- How can it help to think of your story as part of a larger, grander story?
- What connects your story to God's story?
- Where do you find meaning in life? What do you feel you are seeking or searching for in your life right now?

CHAPTER 11

PREPARING THE WAY
JOHN THE BAPTIST

Little Zech. Can you believe that's the name most of my family thought I should have? In my day, you were named after your father, and then your role was to grow into your name. I was to be Zechariah, son of Zechariah, of the Levite tribe, a priest in the Temple like my dad. But that wasn't to be my story.

My mom stood her ground against the rest of the family and named me John. My dad couldn't speak at the time. John, though, was the name the angel Gabriel told my dad to give me. John the Baptist, as you now know me.

I'm not exactly what you expected, am I? People hear the stories of the animal skins I wear and the honey and locusts I eat and they make me out to be a cross between a cave man and a hermit. I do live on the land, and intentionally apart from the influence of the Roman Empire, but I'm not wild. I just don't want to give in to the power of Rome as I've witnessed so many others do. I was raised to be faithful.

I was a miracle baby. Born to be a prophet, or at least that's what my mom and dad told me again and again as I was growing up. When I was a kid, my parents read from the Holy Book, God's word, every day. I learned the words of the Torah and the words of the prophets. Then, I watched as the Jewish leaders began to surrender holiness and right living to pacify the powers of Rome. I had a front row seat because of my dad's role in the Temple. I read God's words about justice and holiness, and then watched as the Pharisees and the scholars traded out the instructions of God that didn't fit their new lifestyle with Roman money and influence. I didn't set out to be a prophet. I shared what God's word said. I just shared what I saw around me. And then, strange things happened: things that I couldn't explain. Wisdom came to me that I didn't learn. Words came to me that didn't start in my brain.

The instructions of God invite us to give our whole lives to Him. They call again and again for us to turn back to God anytime we've turned away. That invitation is always there. That's what I wanted people to know. That we'd lost the story God invites us to be a part of.

The Pharisees had pursued radical personal holiness, but somewhere along the way lost compassion for people. The Sadducees had thrown in their lot with the Roman Empire, and put loyalty to Caesar above commitment to God.

So, I invited people to join me at the Jordan River, to bathe in the water as a symbol of being cleansed from our sins, and to renew our desire to look again to God. And people came. Lots of people came. Lots and lots of people came to see me. Some said it seemed like everyone from Judea and the surrounding countryside. All these people knew things in the world weren't right. They knew. And they'd ask what they should do. And so I shared.

"Anyone who has two shirts should share with the one who has none, and anyone who has food should do the same," I told them.

Tax collectors came and asked what they should do. And I told them, "Don't collect any more than you are required to." Soldiers came and asked what they should do. "Don't extort money and don't accuse people falsely," I told them. I told everyone, "Live by God's instructions." I think I knew these words could be dangerous, could land my head on a platter, because living by God's instructions meant living at odds with the ways of Herod and Antipas and the Jewish leaders of the time who appeased the Empire and taxed people for their own lavish lifestyles and selfish gain. There was that, and, with more and more followers, I was becoming a threat.

In fact, as more people came, they began to ask if I was Elijah. To be honest, I was flattered. Elijah was a mighty prophet. But no, I wasn't doing any miracles. I was just sharing what God's word said.

Then people began to ask if I was the messiah. "No, no," I told them. I'd heard the stories of the messiah from my mom. I knew the time was near. I told them the messiah is coming. And when the messiah comes, I won't even be worthy to tie his sandals.

In fact, I quoted the prophet Isaiah because his words seemed to capture what God was asking me to do: "A voice of one calling in the wilderness, prepare the way for the Lord, make straight paths for him."

"Prepare the way for the Lord." You know, hope is a strange thing. People think of hope as something some people somehow just have and others don't. But hope isn't passive. Hope doesn't magically appear. Hope is active. Hope is a way of living. Hope is living with the expectation that God is going to show up and set things right, even when it doesn't seem like things are right in the moment. Hope is standing up and living for what is right and just even while such living is persecuted or ridiculed. Hope is preparing the way for the Lord because you know the Lord is going to show up. That's why people wanted to be baptized. They wanted to know there was a way to a different future than the oppression and division offered up by the Roman Empire and by leaders who sold out their faith to that empire. They wanted to know there was something they could do. They wanted to hope.

So, I told them there was something to do. "Prepare the way." I would baptize them with water, a sign from the Torah of cleansing – of being forgiven of sins. And once cleansed, they could live again with hope that when the messiah comes, their hearts would be right with God and they would recognize him. And I told them, when the messiah comes, he would baptize with the Holy Spirit.

"Prepare the way," I told them. "Focus your heart on the right things – on God, on caring for others, on justice." Hope, because the messiah will come.

REFLECTION GUIDE & QUESTIONS

- What is something you hope for?

We often think of John the Baptist as a cross between a cave man and a hermit, unkempt with wild hair and a diet of bugs. The references in Matthew's Gospel to his clothing and diet, however, have a different message for a Jewish audience. John the Baptist was acting like Elijah. In fact, you might say that he was wearing an Elijah costume. Why? From his birth, John was given the role of preparing the way for the messiah. Just like Elijah, he was called to challenge the leadership of the time for their hypocrisy and injustice.

- If Elijah or John the Baptist were here today, what actions and behaviors would they confront?

Calling out the hypocrisy of political and religious leaders was a big task! It requires courage and hope. Hope is standing up and living for what is right and just, even while such living is persecuted or ridiculed. Hope is preparing the way for the Lord because you know the Lord is going to show up.

- What do you think it means to "prepare the way for the Lord" (NIV)?
- If John was giving you ways to turn your life back toward God, what instructions would he give you?
- How do we live hopeful lives?
- What is one way that you can commit to living a life of hope?

WHAT'S NEXT

YOUR STORY

When I was a kid, my church never put on a Christmas pageant: I never put on a costume and pretended to be an angel or a wise person or a sheep. Instead, our children's ministry program sang an assortment of songs in "Big Church" during the Advent season. "Go Tell it on the Mountain," "Hark! The Herald Angels Sing," and "Angels We Have Heard on High" were selected nearly every year. There's something sweet and funny, I suppose, about listening to small children try to sing *Gloria, in excelsis Deo*!

I used to feel like I was missing out on this church tradition, that surely I would have made an excellent shepherd or a very tranquil Mary, cradling a baby doll in my arms. As I grew older, though, I came to appreciate that my earliest identities *didn't* end up getting caught in playing a pageant role for my first half-dozen Christmases. I could see myself more completely represented in the fullness of the Advent stories as the years came and went.

The Advent narratives you've read feature unremarkable, ordinary people who God used in remarkable, extraordinary ways. Mary and Joseph were peasants, yet God chose them to carry and care for Christ. Anna was widowed at a young age, relying on her religious community to meet her needs, and proclaimed the birth of her Savior. The magi, like so many of us, were simply looking up at the sky, seeking evidence of God's vastness in the natural world. Perhaps you can see yourself in one or many of these characters, in their longing and in their waiting; in their deep doubt and in their reluctance; in their hopefulness and in their praise. Centuries may have passed between them and us, but our stories, at their core, are intricately connected.

It wasn't until I started working on the chapter featuring Elizabeth that I realized how much like her I really am. In her prayer for a miracle child, I could recognize my own story and my own pain-filled prayers. In some ways, Elizabeth's narrative became autobiographical. She found joy in her service to God and her faith community; in similar ways I have felt no greater joy than in my service to God and to my own church community. Though thousands of years span between Elizabeth and me, my story and her story – and thousands of other women's stories – reveal surprising parallels, held together in the never-ending comforting presence of God.

I accepted an invitation to help write these narratives in part to give a female voice to an old story that has lots of male voices. In the reading and in the writing, I experienced this reminder from God, through Elizabeth's story, that Advent is a story for all of us. And not just in the way that we think of Christ as the light for the whole world, but also that, through connecting our stories with those in the Bible, we are all tied to the same threads of love that God has woven throughout all of humanity from the beginning of time. Once we see our own thread as part of the tapestry, our connection to the story – and our connection to God – grows richer and deeper.

These stories are for all of us, no matter in which chapter you have found yourself. At their core, these are a collective story with roots in God's provision and grace through Jesus: the birth of Christ is for all of humanity, for every person, for the whole world. This is a remarkable reminder of God's presence within our stories.

For many years of my life, I felt a certain affinity for the shepherds keeping watch over their flocks by night. In fact, it was only in recent years I learned that possibly half of the shepherds in the first century were girls. Perhaps I was taught – or perhaps I had always assumed from movies and nativity sets – that shepherding was the work of men. In a staff meeting during the Advent season, though, my senior pastor presented this information on shepherdesses as though it was simply a fun fact. I wanted to press pause on the conversation, but we had already moved on. I think I stared at him, eyes wide, possibly open-mouthed, and not hearing anything else that he said after that.

For me, this "fun fact" tossed out during our weekly staff meeting struck a very important chord. I had just recently had a conversation with a congregation member, a middle-aged woman, who shared that she had, for much of her adult life, struggled to see her place in the gospels. Her church experiences as a young adult were not unlike mine: we had both wrestled with traditions and prescribed gender and cultural roles. In my conversation with her, she talked about the years of personal growth and bible study she had done to make room for herself in the greater gospel story, and especially her place in it as a woman. In her study, she realized the liberating power of Christ in His ministry for and to the oppressed.

Learning that this life-altering and history-making news about the Messiah's birth was first shared with these very shepherds – already social outcasts – took on a wholly deeper meaning when I learned that half of those shepherds keeping watch over flocks at night were most likely teenage girls, the lowest of the low. Christ comes close to the marginalized. God delights in those whom the rest of the world has forgotten: the lost sheep, the dirty shepherd, the lowly woman.

These are stories that show us just a glimpse – a slice – of the fullness of God's love, even for those whose communities have forgotten them, or to those who feel they have been abandoned. The Advent stories are full of mystery, hope, and delight; and all of this goodness is for each of us. Just as each of these characters are incredibly ordinary, God's intended purpose for them was anything but that. These shepherds, though nameless, are the first to declare all that they had seen and heard. Mary is a poor girl in an otherwise-forgotten place, and yet God uses her to prophesy. Joseph, the traditional breadwinner, lays down his pride and his reputation for his betrothed's holy-ordained assignment from God.

You, God's masterpiece, are a living testament to the saving grace of our Lord Jesus Christ. When you revisit the wholeness of the Advent story, I pray you see your part in this grand vision of God's plan, too, no matter your past or your experiences. You are created in the fullness of God and your story is just as unremarkably remarkable as any of these. Many of the lives we encounter in the Advent story were changed by God in moments; I trust that God can and God does use everyday moments for the goodness of God's Kingdom. May you know that you, too, are seen and loved by a God who is more powerful than disease, marginalization, catastrophe, or even death. May you realize that you are seen, loved, and rescued by a God who has proven faithful to these promises.

- Carolyn

SCRIPTURE REFERENCES AND OTHER RESOURCES

Except where otherwise noted, Scripture references are from the New International Version, and unless quoting Scripture directly, the authors have chosen to use gender-neutral language for God.

CHAPTER 1 – HERE I AM: ISAIAH

The authors are grateful to the BEMA Podcast by Marty Solomon for his material on the Prophet Isaiah, and especially for his commentary on the six woes of Isaiah 5.

Some concepts for this chapter were inspired by *The Prophets* by Abraham J. Heschel.

Isaiah 6:3 – "Holy, holy, holy is the Lord Almighty; the whole earth is full of his glory."

In Moses' encounter with God in Exodus 33:19-20, God says that no one can see God's face and live.

Isaiah 6:8-13 describes God's selection of Isaiah and Isaiah's response.

Isaiah 7:3 references Isaiah's son.

If you would like to explore more about King Ahaz and his interactions with the Prophet Isaiah, you can learn more in Isaiah chapters 7-9.

Isaiah 7:14 – "The young woman is pregnant and is about to give birth to a son, and she will name him

Immanuel" (CEB). Note that the NIV and other translations use "virgin" instead of "young woman." The CEB and NRSV do not denote the young woman in the passage as a virgin.

Isaiah 11:6-9 – "The wolf will live with the lamb…"

Isaiah 9:6-7 – "For to us a child is born…"

Isaiah chapters 52 and 53 are often referred to as the suffering servant passage. While this passage is equated with Jesus, Isaiah was speaking to those who were suffering in exile for the sins of those who came before.

Isaiah 12:2-5 – "Surely God is my salvation…"

CHAPTER 2 – EXPECTING MIRACLES: ZECHARIAH

Proverbs 3:5-6 – "Trust in the Lord with all your heart, and lean not on your own understanding."

Isaiah 59:20 – "The Redeemer will come to Zion, to those in Jacob who repent of their sins, thus says the Lord."

Zechariah and Elizabeth's lineage is mentioned in Luke 1:5-7.

1 Chronicles 23 explains David appointing the Levites to the priesthood.

For more on Zechariah's experience in the Holy of Holies, see Luke 1:8-23.

To read Zechariah's song, see Luke 1:67-80.

CHAPTER 3 – PURE JOY: ELIZABETH

Childlessness was considered a great rebuke and punishment from God for women. For more, see Genesis 18, Genesis 25, Genesis 30, and 1 Samuel 1.

Psalm 30:5 – "Weeping may stay for the night, but in the morning, joy."

While biblical scholars disagree on whether men could divorce their wives for any reason they saw fit, it is true that only men could initiate a divorce. For more on this topic, visit Deuteronomy 24:1-4.

Like Elizabeth, Hannah struggled to conceive her son Samuel. To read about Hannah's commitment of Samuel to God, see 1 Samuel 1:1-2 and 1:19-28.

Luke 1:42 – "Blessed are you among women, and blessed is the child you will bear!" To read about Mary and Elizabeth's reunion, see Luke 1:39-45.

Luke 1:60 – "His name will be John, for God is gracious!" To read more about John's birth and naming, see Luke 1:57-66.

In Genesis 4, Eve says, "With the help of God, I have brought forth a man."

Genesis 30:23 – "The Lord has taken away my shame."

Genesis 18:14 – "Is anything too difficult for the Lord?" These words are spoken to Sarah from a messenger of God upon sharing with Abraham that Sarah will have a baby in her old age.

CHAPTER 4: I AM THE LORD'S: MARY

The indented subsections in Mary's chapter are lines from Mary's Song, also called the Magnificat, in Luke 1:46-55 (see also cross reference to 1 Samuel 2:1-10).

To read more about Mary's divine encounter, see Luke 1:26-38.

For more on Moses' experience with God at Horeb (also known as Sinai), see Exodus 17.

Although we don't know for certain if stoning was used as a punishment for an impure bride, Deuteronomy 22:13-21 lists the consequences for non-virgin women who enter into marriage.

Luke 1:38 – "I am the Lord's servant. May your word to me be fulfilled."

CHAPTER 5 – GOD WITH US: JOSEPH

For Jesus' genealogy, read Matthew 1:1-17.

To read about Joseph's dream, see Matthew 1:18-25.

CHAPTER 6 – THE GIFT OF PEACE: AN INTERLUDE FROM GABRIEL

To read about Daniel's experiences with Gabriel, see Daniel 8:15-27 and 9:20-23.

Read more about contact with angels in Isaiah 6, Ezekiel 10, and Revelation 4.

For more stories on human contact with angels, see Genesis 16 (Hagar), Judges 6 (Gideon), Daniel 10 (Daniel), and Luke 1 (Zechariah and Mary).

Luke 1:13 – "Do not be afraid, Zechariah; your prayer has been heard."

Luke 1:28 – "Greetings, you who are highly favored! The Lord is with you." (See Luke 1:26-38.)

"Peace on earth, goodwill to all humanity." The authors have opted for gender-neutral terminology for this interpretation of Luke 2:14.

CHAPTER 7 – A PROMISE: A SHEPHERD

For the full biblical account of the angels' visit to the shepherds, read Luke 2:8-20.

To read about David's ascent from shepherd to throne, see 1 & 2 Samuel.

The angels' song appears in Luke 2:13-14.

Some creative concepts about the role of the shepherd caring for the firstborn lamb are drawn from *Jesus: A Theography* by Leonard Sweet and Frank Viola.

For more on Jesus' background in Galilee and Nazareth, read Luke 4:14-22.

CHAPTER 8 – MAKING ROOM: THE INNKEEPER

Though the Innkeeper is a fictional character added to modern retellings of the Christmas story, one can imagine his reaction to having a census take place in Bethlehem. To read the biblical account of the census, see Luke 2:1-7.

To read what the prophets say regarding the birth of Immanuel, see Micah 5:2, Isaiah 7:14, and Isaiah 9:7.

CHAPTER 9 – GOOD NEWS: SIMEON AND ANNA

The full biblical account of Simeon, Anna, and Jesus' presentation at the Temple is explained in Luke 2:22-40.

Luke's Gospel says that Anna was 84 years old at the time of Jesus' birth (see Luke 2:36-37).

See Luke 2:25-26 for a description of Simeon's message from the Holy Spirit.

Luke 2:30-32 – "For my eyes have seen your salvation…"

Luke 2:35b – "A sword will pierce your own soul, too."

Luke 2:38 describes Anna sharing about the redemption of Jerusalem with those whom she encountered.

CHAPTER 10 – THE STORY DOESN'T BEGIN HERE: A WISE MAN

To read the full account of the magis' visit, see Matthew 2:1-12.

Information about the Star of Bethlehem was drawn from the article, "The Star of Bethlehem: Can science explain what it really was?" by Eric Betz. Published on astronomy.com on December 23, 2023.

Numbers 24:15-17 includes the reference to the star: "...a star shall come forth out of Jacob, and a scepter shall rise out of Israel."

Isaiah 9:2 – "The people who walk in darkness will see a great light; Those who live in a dark land, the light will shine on them."

See Isaiah 9, Jeremiah 23, and Micah 5 for a few examples of God's promises through the prophets.

King Herod famously built the Herodion, a fantastic hilltop palace named after himself, during the years 23-15 BCE. The palace included gardens, a bathhouse, and a theater among other amenities.

Daniel 7:13-14 (NRSV) – "I saw one like a human being coming with the clouds of heaven..."

CHAPTER 11 – PREPARING THE WAY: JOHN THE BAPTIST

To learn more about the birth and naming of John the Baptist, see Luke 1:57-66.

Matthew 3:4 and Mark 1:6 describe John's lifestyle, including clothing and dietary choices.

Zechariah's song identifies Jewish identity, the challenges of society, and John's role to prepare the way for Christ. See Luke 1:67-80.

To read more about Jesus' conflicts with the Pharisees and Sadducees, explore Matthew 20, Matthew 22, Matthew 23, and Luke 11.

John baptized many people, including Jesus. To read the account of Jesus' baptism, see Matthew 3:13-17, Mark 1:9-11, and Luke 3:21-22.

Luke 3:11 – "Anyone who has two shirts should share with the one who has none, and anyone who has food should do the same."

Luke 3:13 – "Don't collect any more than you are required to."

Luke 3:14 – "Don't extort money and don't accuse people falsely."

Matthew 14:1-12 tells the account of John the Baptist's death.

Isaiah 40:3 – "A voice of one calling in the wilderness, prepare the way for the Lord, make straight paths for him."

www.ingramcontent.com/pod-product-compliance
Ingram Content Group UK Ltd.
Pitfield, Milton Keynes, MK11 3LW, UK
UKHW032333131224
452011UK00004B/51